THE DIRT DIRECTORY

HANNAH COLLINGRIDGE

THE DIRT DIRECTORY

The ultimate guide to the UK's bike parks, trail centres and purpose-built mountain biking trails

Vertebrate Publishing, Sheffield
www.adventurebooks.com

THE DIRT DIRECTORY
HANNAH COLLINGRIDGE

First published in 2025 by Vertebrate Publishing

VERTEBRATE PUBLISHING
Omega Court, 352 Cemetery Road, Sheffield S11 8FT, United Kingdom.
www.adventurebooks.com

Copyright © Hannah Collingridge 2025.

Front cover: BikePark Wales. © Andy Lloyd/BikePark Wales.
Individual photography as credited.

Hannah Collingridge has asserted her rights under the Copyright, Designs and Patents Act 1988 to be identified as author of this work.

A CIP catalogue record for this book is available from the British Library.

ISBN 978-1-83981-128-9 (Paperback)
ISBN 978-1-83981-129-6 (Ebook)

All rights reserved. No part of this work covered by the copyright herein may be reproduced or used in any form or by any means – graphic, electronic, or mechanised, including photocopying, recording, taping or information storage and retrieval systems – without the written permission of the publisher.

Every effort has been made to obtain the necessary permissions with reference to copyright material, both illustrative and quoted. We apologise for any omissions in this respect and will be pleased to make the appropriate acknowledgements in any future edition.

Vertebrate Publishing is committed to printing on paper from sustainable sources.

Printed and bound in Slovenia by Latitude Press.

Every effort has been made to achieve accuracy of the information in this guidebook. The author, publisher and copyright owners can take no responsibility for: loss or injury (including fatal) to persons; loss or damage to property or equipment; trespass, irresponsible behaviour nor any other mishap that may be suffered as a result of following the route descriptions or advice offered in this guidebook. The inclusion of a track or path as part of a route, or otherwise recommended, in this guidebook does not guarantee that the track or path will remain a right of way. If conflict with landowners arises we advise that you act politely and leave by the shortest route available. If the matter needs to be taken further then please take it up with the relevant authority.

CONTENTS

Introduction *p7*
    Acknowledgements *p7*

About this book *p8*
    What it covers *p8*
    What it doesn't cover *p8*
    What's a trail centre? *p8*
    And what's a bike park? *p9*
    Trail grading *p9*
    Trail maintenance *p10*
    Trail conditions *p11*
    What bike? *p11*
    Protection *p11*
    Trail safety and etiquette *p12*
    To the trails *p13*
    Online resources *p13*

South East England *p17*
South West England *p27*
The Midlands & East Anglia *p43*
Yorkshire & the Humber *p61*
Northern England *p79*
Wales *p95*
Scotland *p125*
Northern Ireland *p165*

Glossary *p172*
Top Tens *p174*

INTRODUCTION

Trail centres with designated, waymarked trails have been around in the UK since the late 1990s. Since then, they have gone through considerable changes in the way they are built and the style of riding – and rider – they cater for. There are certain trail builders who can date a trail and tell you who built it, much as others might date a piece of architecture. The historiography of how riding and bike fashions have changed in the last 25 years would be another piece of writing entirely, but it does mean that now there is a wider than ever variety of purpose-built and waymarked places to ride your bike. The aim of this book is to give you a nudge in the right direction to find something you will enjoy riding.

Why ride at a trail centre or a bike park? For one, it's easy: you turn up and follow a series of arrows and you have a ride. You're likely to know the kind of riding you'll encounter and the distance involved, plus quite often there's the opportunity for a brew and cake at the end. You might fancy riding a particular sort of trail, such as a jump line, and if you pick the right place you get the ride you want. Riding at a trail centre or bike park is very different from following a map and a bridleway, just as coffee and tea are different and you can fancy one thing at one time and the other sometime else. There's also nothing stopping you using a trail centre trail as part of a longer ride.

There are also no access issues to worry about which, until all of the UK catches up with the Scottish Outdoor Access Code, makes it easy to know you have a legitimate right to ride there. Indeed, if you combine trail centres and bike parks with our rights of way system, we've never had so many good places to ride.

Off you go. Go and ride them.

ACKNOWLEDGEMENTS

As ever, many other people have contributed immensely to the writing of this book. Thanks go to the ever-supportive team at Vertebrate Publishing for encouragement and distraction, probably in equal measure; Joolze Dymond who rode with me so often, took pictures and was a handy measure of how gnarly a trail was getting; the many, many people I have chatted to online, via email and sometimes in actual real life – there are far too many to name but you have all been incredibly helpful; Richie Rowland of Mondraker lent me a (very nice) bike when I was in need; Rory Hitchens (then) of Upgrade Bikes allowed me to play on a (orange) prototype Kinesis UK; Schwalbe tyres supplied rubbery goodness for all occasions; Matt Holstead of Arrow Bike Wheels kept them straight and true; Torq Fitness supplied the snacks; Alpkit helped with riding kit; Matt Williams and the Run & Ride crew in Milford let me raid the shop relatively uncomplainingly; Paul Davis taught me so much about trails, building and flow, and let me borrow his ebike frequently. All stars.

Those who have been an inspiration in terms of riding but also for conversations about riding and getting more folk doing it: Aneela McKenna and the FNY crew; Jenni Gwiazdowski for spannering chat; Kathy Gilchrist, the first female president of Scottish Cycling; Claire Bennett and the Hope WMN; Rich Martin and the crew at Cyclewise; the Saint Piran family; and the RR23 team.

And, as always, my family, who brought me up to be this way; my wife who appreciates the peace and quiet – and tidiness – when I'm away; and my friends, notably the Garage Bikes crew, the other, slightly chunkier Team GB. Team Satsuma forever.

OPPOSITE BIKEPARK WALES. © ANDY LLOYD/BIKEPARK WALES

THE DIRT DIRECTORY

GLENTRESS. © ANDY McCANDLISH

ABOUT THIS BOOK

This book is designed to be a reference volume covering all the (known!) trail centres and bike parks in the United Kingdom. Obviously, this is a constantly shifting topic to write about, so always check the place still exists, is open and isn't suffering from storm damage before you go. The book gives information about the facilities such as parking, toilets and refreshments and so on available, or not, at the trailhead, as well as a brief guide to the trails found there. Hopefully that is enough information for you to decide whether you fancy riding there. Be aware that some facilities, especially cafes, may well be seasonal.

TRAIL CENTRES
BIKE PARKS

- Parking
- Toilets
- Refreshments
- Bike shop
- Bike hire
- Uplift

WHAT IT COVERS

Purpose-built, waymarked trails. Somewhere you can turn up at without having been to the area before and find a trail to ride without needing to navigate. This does mean that a lot of places which are great to ride but aren't waymarked are omitted, most notably in Scotland.

WHAT IT DOESN'T COVER

Unmarked and unsanctioned trails. These are liable to disappear either due to forestry operations or lack of use, plus there are potential liability and insurance issues. Where there is accepted riding near to a centre, possibly due to a local trail-management group such as the Tweed Valley Trails Association and the Golfie (p138), it will be mentioned. However, even these trails are likely to disappear at some point, so check your information before you travel.

Also, there isn't a full list of pump tracks, just because there are so many.

WHAT'S A TRAIL CENTRE?

For years this was what waymarked mountain biking was all about. Usually on Forestry Commission (FC) land, you'd have trails laid out through a wood. There are still lots of these

ABOUT THIS BOOK

throughout the UK and usually you only pay for car parking, which in turn helps support trail maintenance. FC, under its various names, tends to play safe and is mostly pretty risk averse (there are some exceptions), so the gnarliest riding isn't usually found in their woods as waymarked trails. The quality of the riding, and amount of singletrack versus fire road, can depend on when the trails were built and what the fashion was for trails at the time, so it can depend on your favoured style of riding whether you'll find a place fun. FC trails also change very slowly, as permissions and funding are so slow to take effect. But one advantage is that they are usually always open.

AND WHAT'S A BIKE PARK?

This is the phrase I've used to refer to sites where you likely need to book (best done in advance) and sign a waiver of some sort before you are allowed to ride. Most of these places are privately owned and there is usually a slant towards harder, more technical riding. I have split bike parks into two flavours: the gravity, downhill (DH), enduro side of things; and the smooth, flowy tracks with big jumps, although some places do both. Bike parks tend to cater for the gnarlier sort of riding grades, because you have acknowledged the inherent risks of mountain biking in the waiver. And because bike parks are largely built on private land, they have much more freedom to develop and change their lines – without doubt the majority of the bike parks listed here will have changed by the time the book goes to print, hence some of the listings for bike parks are more descriptive than absolute. However, most sites are pretty clued up about keeping information on their social media up to date. A warning about social media: some pro riders regularly use certain bike parks and will post videos on YouTube, etc. These people are pro for a reason – they ride much, much better and harder than the rest of us. Do not necessarily be put off by their rides. Instead, look for videos of normal riders spooning and casing the same jumps – that will give you a much better idea of what a bike park really rides like. Also remember that video flattens everything, so be prepared for stuff being steeper than you might have thought on the screen; if it looks steep on a GoPro, it's probably vertical in reality. Bike parks are likely to have restricted opening hours: some close during the week, some in the winter. Check before you travel.

TRAIL GRADING

There is a great variety of purpose-built riding in the UK, and therefore there is a means of labelling the routes so you know roughly – sometimes very roughly – what you are heading into.

First, to be included in this book, a trail has to be a purpose-built MTB trail. Many forests have blue routes that just stay on fire roads – these are not described. Nor are the green family routes, unless they are one of the very rare beasts that are purpose-built, wide singletrack perfect for beginners of any age and ideal for building confidence. Where a forest has family routes as well as MTB routes, they are listed. Also, a couple of routes on easy trails are randomly graded purple!

■ Blue trails

At trail centres, it is designated that on blue trails all of the features will be rollable, obstacles will be small, and, if tricky, there will usually be another, easier, way around. They will be suitable for kids (and adults) with a bit of off-road confidence, but not so tricky that it would put them off. Generally, blue trails tend to be shorter. A good blue will be suitable for those pottering round slightly nervously, but will also be a lot of fun for more confident riders; a mediocre blue will be fairly boring for all. Some older blue trails are just on fire roads, but are longer than the green trail at the same place, and so these have not been included.

A bike park blue should still have features which are all rollable, but expect it to be more demanding than something at a trail centre. In general with bike parks, it's prudent to start on a grade lower than you ride at a trail centre until you get the feel for that particular bike park. It will also give you a warm-up – always a good thing.

■ Red trails

'Red' covers an extremely broad area, and in some ways it isn't that useful a grading. It can cover gentler cross-country-style routes, which may give you a longer ride but not much in the way of technical challenges, through to trails from the edge of a hillside where the only way down is steep, loose and technical. All of these can be described as 'red', and how happy you are on a trail can depend entirely on your riding style and preferences.

Red trails at bike parks take the difficulty a step further and can incorporate many more technical features that require you to be reasonably proficient and confident to ride well.

To help you further, I have therefore added a bit to the red trail descriptions. Naturally these are subjective, and you may well disagree:

XC: this doesn't have too many technical features but could be a lengthier ride, with the grading relating more to the required fitness level than technical ability. This is how many older trail centres were judged. There may be a fair amount of fire road involved. Something like Dalby Forest (p76) is a classic example of the old-school style of red trail.

Enduro: this is likely to be more technical, with possibly shorter runs designed to be sessioned rather than a long ride out. Reds at bike parks are likely to be steeper and much more technical than those at trail centres, but that is what you are paying for. Reds at jump parks will still likely be rollable, but the features will be bigger and longer. For instance, there will be tables rather than gaps, but the lengths of the tables will have increased.

■ Black trails

At trail centres this is about as hard as it gets. A black trail will contain bigger trail features which may not have a way around – a chicken line – and will therefore require commitment. At bike parks, this commitment could well be a large one. On enduro/DH sites expect drop-offs and jumps that can't be rolled. At this point, protection in terms of pads and full-face helmets is not only a wise precaution but part of the conditions of riding at some places. At jump parks, black trails involve gaps that have to be jumped.

■ Bike parks may also have black plus and pro lines, often graded orange. If you aren't sure about the grading of a place, start with something gentle to get your eye in. Riding something too easy is better than breaking yourself on your first run. It's also less embarrassing.

Dave grading

In reality, no matter the trail centre grading, we all split tracks into one of three grades, which I refer to as *Dave grades*:
1. **Dave friendly:** you are quite happy on this and are not out of your comfort zone.
2. **Mildly terrifying:** there are some sections which push you a bit.
3. **No:** not riding this one.

I cannot know which trails fall into which grade for you – you can argue about it at great length on the internet, though.

TRAIL MAINTENANCE

Trails do not look after themselves and maintenance costs money. There's such a thing as freeride, but there's no such thing as a free ride. Whatever you feel about the funding of the various Forestry Commission divisions, paying for car parking does, in part, contribute to maintenance. If you feel that maintenance could be better, get in touch with the local ranger, find out about dig days and pitch in.

ABOUT THIS BOOK

LADY CANNING'S PLANTATION. © *JOHN COEFIELD*

TARLAND TRAILS. © *SOPHIE FLETCHER*

Find out about local trail groups and support them if you can, either with cash or time.

With bike parks it's a little more obvious where the money goes, and if a bike park doesn't provide good riding it's not going to get repeat customers. Expect trails to change or to be closed for maintenance, and check your information before making a special trip. Storms can damage forests, meaning trails are closed until they can be cleared, and felling of trees can disrupt normal service. Some bike parks close during the winter to protect the trails; other places ask you not to ride there after extremely wet weather.

TRAIL CONDITIONS

Some trails hold water, others drain well; some have gloopy mud, some have really slippery mud. The variety in Britain is pretty wide because of our wide-ranging geology and variable weather. Surfaced trails will generally ride well all year round, even if there are puddles on the trail; more natural-feeling trails could well become greasy and tree roots will be just waiting to take you out. Tyre compound and pressure will make a difference, so read up and be prepared to experiment if you can. If a trail is rocky and wet, it will depend on what rock it is as to how grippy it is. Bear in mind there is not a rubber compound yet invented that will grip on damp chalk.

WHAT BIKE?

Whatever you feel comfortable on. There are limits to what hardtails can deal with, but frankly until you become a very, very good rider the bike will be a lot more capable than you are. That having been said, there are certainly places where full suspension is much more comfortable.

There are very few bad modern mountain bikes, so don't worry if you haven't got this season's required travel – it will change by next year, and what was a good bike last season doesn't stop being good just because it's a year older. Check your bike set-up suits you and go on skills courses to have a professional help you ride better rather than just buying the latest gadget – developing your skills will be much better value for your riding.

Some of these trails are even suitable for gravel bikes, although the rocky sections will be rubbish – and just because you *can*, doesn't mean you *should* …

PROTECTION

Different riders wear different things. What you wear can depend on how hot you get when you are riding, your confidence levels or sometimes whether you've just got used to riding in certain things. It's only when things get gnarly that you might want to add to your normal gear.

THE DIRT DIRECTORY

DALBY FOREST. © *JOHN COEFIELD*

© *JOHN COEFIELD*

In terms of what you might wear:
- **Helmet:** please wear a helmet. Why wouldn't you unless there is a religious reason not to? Off-road helmets tend to have more coverage around the back of the head, but that's not crucial on many trails.
- **Full-face helmet:** some bike parks make it a condition that you wear a full-face helmet and at least knee pads. Be sure to check before you rock up with only a trail helmet. And again, if it makes you feel more confident, crack on. They are very hot to ride uphill in, though.
- **Gloves:** keep the skin on your hands, not the trail. There are so many varieties of gloves available; full-fingered ones tend to be better for gnarlier stuff.
- **Baggy shorts/long trousers:** not just because it's what MTBers wear, but because they offer an extra layer of protection. There's a reason downhillers ride in full sleeves.
- **Knee pads/arm pads:** there are plenty of trail pads now that can be worn reasonably comfortably all day. If they make you feel more confident, put them on. If you have uplift booked, you may choose to wear something sturdier as you don't have to worry about pedalling in them.
- **Spine/back/hip protection:** these are advisable for the really gnarly stuff, but again it depends on personal preference.

No equipment can keep you entirely safe and hurt-free, but it can likely mitigate the effects of crashing. Don't forget, if you hit your head during a crash, replace your helmet – it has done its job and now has a weak spot where you hit it. Many manufacturers have crash replacement schemes which are worth checking out.

TRAIL SAFETY AND ETIQUETTE

Here are some suggestions for looking after yourself and others when you are riding. We are all out for a nice ride, whatever that means to you, so kindness and respect will help everyone.
- 'Be nice, say hi' is the single best piece of advice for all activities in life, including riding bikes.
- Leave the trails as you found them, or in even better condition. Pick up bits of litter where you can. Not all of it will have been dropped deliberately – someone may just have missed their pocket with a wrapper, so we can all help each other a bit here.
- If a trail is closed, DO NOT RIDE IT. It's closed for a reason, whether it's blocked, unsafe, being rebuilt, whatever. You are helping no one by riding it.
- Offer help to other riders if they look like they might need it, whether that be tools, help, directions – whatever you've got.

ABOUT THIS BOOK

- If you come up behind a slower rider and would like to get past, then give a friendly greeting and ask something like, 'When you are ready, can I get past please?' and give them room to ride. Don't buzz them or pass comment on their riding.
- If someone is behind you and asks to come past, acknowledge their friendly greeting and reply that you'll pull over as soon as you can for them. Pull over when you are able and are comfortable to do so.
- Don't stop in the middle of the track (unless you've crashed there). Pull off the riding line properly. If you are in a group, make sure you are all off the line.
- If you or your riding buddy has crashed, then protect the trail if they cannot be moved. Walk back up the trail to warn other riders and place an upside-down bike across the trail in a place where it can be clearly seen and where oncoming riders have time to stop.
- If you see an upside-down bike on the trail, it means there is an obstruction on the track ahead. Proceed with caution.
- Take enough stuff with you to get out of any situations you might get into. Can you look after yourself if something happens? On the other hand, don't take stuff you don't know how to use. If you are on a group ride it can make sense to share the stuff out among you, so you aren't all carrying all of the things.
- There may be horses in the same woods you are riding in (not likely in bike parks). Speak to them and their rider. Horses tend to respond to human voices and may realise that the scary thing near them has a human voice and therefore isn't quite as scary. The noise of your freehub may well spook them, so be prepared to pedal very slowly past them so the hub is engaged. And let the rider work out how you pass each other – they are familiar with their horse and know how it is reacting. As a rule of thumb, horses with their ears forward are generally happier than those with their ears back. Be prepared to stop if you see ears suddenly flicking backwards.
- If you come across livestock on the trails, don't chase or frighten them even if it stops your run. That's someone's livelihood there.

TO THE TRAILS

The country is split up into regions/countries in this book to make it easier for you to find somewhere to ride. Some places have more structured riding than others, and some areas seem to have more of one sort of riding than another, usually to do with the number of hills available.

Trail centres are colour-coded **GREEN**; bike parks are **PINK** and will usually have an emphasis on enduro/DH or jump lines, although many have both.

Most importantly, have fun while you are riding. Remember not to take it too seriously – it's going into the woods to play on your bike.

ONLINE RESOURCES

dmbins.com – the Developing Mountain Biking in Scotland page has a wealth of information about all kinds of off-road riding in Scotland.

forestryandland.gov.scot/visit/activities/mountain-biking – up-to-date information about closures on Forestry and Land Scotland land.

www.mountainbikeni.com – this covers Northern Ireland.

www.forestryengland.uk/cycling – a site for cycling in English forests.

www.mbwales.com – information about MTB in Wales.

www.trailforks.com – information about trail centres, but also other trails.

THE DIRT DIRECTORY

THE DIRT DIRECTORY

TARLAND TRAILS. © *ANDY McCANDLISH*

SOUTH EAST ENGLAND

The South East may not have the big hills of other areas in the UK, but it does have plenty of stuff to ride all year round. Slippery chalk is more of an issue than mud in certain areas, but if jumps are your thing, there is an amazing choice of venues.

1. Southampton Bike Park *p20*
2. Queen Elizabeth Country Park *p20*
3. Rogate Downhill B1KEPARK *p20*
4. Swinley Forest *p21*
5. S4P B1KEPARK *p22*
6. Surrey Hills – Leith Hill *p22*
7. Deers Leap Park *p23*
8. Bull Track Bike Park *p23*
9. Bedgebury National Pinetum and Forest *p23*
10. Friston Forest *p24*
11. Betteshanger Park *p24*
12. Redbridge Cycling Centre *p24*
13. Lee Valley VeloPark *p24*
14. Aston Hill Bike Park *p24*
15. Woburn Sands *p25*

THE DIRT DIRECTORY

SOUTH EAST ENGLAND

ROGATE DOWNHILL B1KEPARK. © *JOOLZE DYMOND*

THE DIRT DIRECTORY

SOUTHAMPTON BIKE PARK

50.9426, -1.4234 / The Outdoor Sports Centre, Thornhill Road, Southampton, Hampshire, SO16 7AY / Trail maintenance: built and maintained by volunteers / www.southamptonbikepark.com

This is a constantly developing small jump park – but while the park is small, not all of the jumps are. It offers a lot of opportunity for progression, with jumps for all ages and abilities. It does get very soggy in wet weather, and is best not ridden at those times.

Trails
There's a start hill, three trails with a dedicated push-up and an advanced jump trail. It's a great local facility.

QUEEN ELIZABETH COUNTRY PARK

50.9614, -0.9778 / South Downs Way, Hampshire, PO8 0QE / Trail maintenance: www.facebook.com/qecptrailbuilding / www.forestryengland.uk/queen-elizabeth-country-park

This is a rightly popular place, with a fantastic blue trail that is excellent for all riders. As it's on chalk, certain parts of the route can get quite slippery in the damp.

There is also plenty of off-piste riding. The wood is well used for local enduro, DH and XC races.

Trails
■ **6-kilometre, award-winning flow trail.**
Like the best blue trails, it can be ridden by the less confident and the beginner, or absolutely nailed by the experienced. It is a long but pleasant climb up and then a swooping, flowy descent with berms and some rollers. Once you have got to the top of the climb it's pretty much downhill all the way. It has the occasional trail feature, but everything is rollable. The berms get bigger the further down the hill you go, so it's great for developing technique.

■ **7 kilometres.** This trail has a fair amount of climbing, but it is made more interesting by short downs every so often. There are longer downs towards the end. This is a natural-feeling trail, so expect roots.

ROGATE DOWNHILL B1KEPARK

51.0275, -0.8664 / Rogate Woods, Combe Hill, Rogate, West Sussex, GU31 5DL / www.b1ke.com/b1keparks/rogate-downhill

In order to ride here you will need to sign up as a free member and then pay for a day pass. Or, for regulars, there is a better-value annual membership for all of the B1KEPARKS. All of the trails involve a push up to the top.

Rogate is known for being rideable all year round due to the sandy nature of the soil, and it's also known for providing a great deal of varied riding within a smallish site, with a whole variety of flow and techy trails. It already has a long history of mountain biking and continues to be developed to match current riding trends. The site is split by a fire road, meaning sessioning can be done on half tracks as well as full. A good place to progress your riding.

The trail grading here involves both the colour of the trail and also a lozenge/dot system to give you further information: a single lozenge means it's a gentler trail and everything can be rolled; two-lozenge trails have bigger features and stuff that it's better not to roll, although alternative lines may be available; three lozenges mean you need to be comfortable and competent with your wheels off the ground. Both the colour grading and lozenge number should give you a reasonable amount of information about the trail but, as always with this kind of place, it's sometimes worth having a good look at features before riding them. There is also plenty of information about the trails on the website.

SOUTH EAST ENGLAND

ROGATE DOWNHILL BIKEPARK. © *JOOLZE DYMOND*

Trails

🟦 **Bottle Rocket.** This is the classic warm-up track, a blue, two-lozenge trail which is described as 'fast, flowy and as rowdy as you want it to be'. In other words, this will give you a great feel of what Rogate is like and how your riding style and skill fits in with the place. Do not be put off by the blue appellation – this is not a trail centre blue. There are a lot of very good riders who come here, such as Sam Reynolds, Olly Wilkins et al., and they warm up on the blue. Point taken? After this, it's a case of working your way upwards.

Other trails include a variety of flow and tech trails. Have a look at the trail map and descriptions: expect roots, rocks, drops and turns of all kinds. There are some very big features here such as the DMR whale tail and some very large tables and doubles.

Trails

🟩 **1 kilometre.** This trail is made up of gently rolling, wider singletrack. It's one way so is great for families and beginners, and it is a good trail on which to start building off-road confidence.

🟦 **9 kilometres.** Undulating, flowy trail with not too much linking fire road. There are some berms and rollers but nothing too technical, so it is a good beginner trail.

🟥 **14 kilometres,** plus the blue trail to get there and back. This is sort of a figure of eight off the blue, so if you overestimate things you can cut it shorter. As with the blue, this is an undulating, flowy trail but with more technical features, plus some jumps and drops.

Other features

There is also the area known as The Summit, a purpose-built, private skills area. You will need to pay to use this area (*www.swinleybikehub.com/coaching*) but it should cover any and all areas of riding you need to improve, from beginners and basics through to big jumps and drops.

SWINLEY FOREST

51.3874, -0.7411 / Nine Mile Ride, Bracknell, Berkshire, RG12 7QW / Trail maintenance: Swinley Bike Hub / *www.swinleybikehub.com*

Handily close to London, Swinley Forest offers a good variety of riding, especially for families and beginners.

THE DIRT DIRECTORY

SURREY HILLS – LEITH HILL. © *JANE BEAGLEY*

S4P B1KEPARK

51.1698, -0.6586 / Godalming, Surrey, GU8 5BJ / www.b1ke.com/b1keparks/s4p-milford

Although riding on this site is free, you will need to sign up for free as a member of B1KEPARKS to ride here. This ensures insurance requirements are met, both for you and the bike park. Although it's called a bike park, it's essentially a set of dirt jumps that no one makes any money out of, so don't be shy about pitching in to help with maintenance.

    Sam Reynolds, Brendan Fairclough and Olly Wilkins, among others, ride here regularly as well as helping to build and maintain it. That's how good the jumps are.

Trails

This is entirely a jump park – there are no trails – but it is designed to be progressive, so there's a line of rollers, a line of tables, a line of doubles and then trick jumps of a larger nature. It's built on sand, so not only does it ride well in most weathers, but also crashing isn't as painful as it could be. Obviously, it's designed to be sessioned.

SURREY HILLS – LEITH HILL

51.1764, -0.3712 / Leith Hill Tower, Dorking, Surrey, RH5 6LX / www.surreyhillsmountainbiking.co.uk

Surrey Hills is an area rather than one specific spot, with lots of riding but only one waymarked trail. However, there are access agreements in place in some of the woods to allow riding on the built-up trails, and there are plenty of bridleways in the area too. See *www.surreyhillsmountainbiking.co.uk* for lots of suggestions. Be aware of the access agreements, carefully negotiated and agreed for the area, and don't ride in a way which might jeopardise those agreements for everyone else. The area gets very busy at weekends, so bear this in mind when planning where to park.

Trails

■ **Summer Lightning – 7.3 kilometres as a loop.**

    There are loads and loads of absolutely amazing trails here, they just aren't waymarked, so grab a map or chat to a local and go exploring. The trails are mostly of the loamy, flowy

SOUTH EAST ENGLAND

variety and some have reached legendary status locally. There are some big jumps here and there too. It's pretty sandy under wheel, so usually rides well all year round.

DEERS LEAP PARK

51.1047, -0.0231 / Saint Hill Green, East Grinstead, West Sussex, RH19 4NG

Temporarily closed until spring 2026 for redevelopment. The info below relates to the site pre-closure.

Deers Leap is a small park that's aimed at beginners and families. You will need to sign on and pay at the bike shop before you ride. Most stuff is very novice and child friendly. There's also pond dipping on site, and they cater for school parties and youth groups.

Trails
🟩/🟦 **5 kilometres.** The main trail has slightly harder lines than elsewhere in the wood. It's great for families and has no unexpected obstacles.

Other features
🟧 There is a skills park, pump track and some North Shore. Lots for kids (of all ages) to have a go at.

BULL TRACK BIKE PARK

51.0516, 0.1949 / Palesgate Lane, Crowborough, East Sussex, TN6 3HF / *thebulltrack.co.uk*

Bull Track Bike Park is a dirt jump and freeride park with a whole range of sizes of jumps, from small tables through to absolutely massive gaps and trick jumps. You'll need to book before going or buy an annual ticket. They also hold an annual jam, and coaching is available.

Trails
This bike park is primarily focused on getting your wheels off the ground, so a full-face

SURREY HILLS – LEITH HILL. © *JANE BEAGLEY*

helmet and body armour are recommended, especially on the bigger stuff. There are plenty of chances for progression here, with smaller lines building up to lines with split options: tables on one side, gaps on the other.

BEDGEBURY NATIONAL PINETUM AND FOREST

51.0719, 0.4467 / Lady Oak Lane, Goudhurst, Kent, TN17 2SJ / *www.forestryengland.uk/bedgebury*

Bedgebury is good for families and beginners, and there are coaching and women-only sessions available on site, too. There is a world-leading collection of conifers if you want to spend time deliberately looking at trees rather than riding past them – there's even a handy search tool for the tree collection at *bedgebury.arboretumexplorer.org*

Trails
🟧 **13 kilometres.** This comprises mixed fire road and hard-packed gravel singletrack, so it weathers well. It is undulating and flowy rather than overly technical, and is good for beginners at the grade. There is one optional black section which has a few drop-offs.

Multi-use trails
🟦 **4.5 and 9 kilometres.** These are family trails.

THE DIRT DIRECTORY

FRISTON FOREST

50.7810, 0.1861
(**50.7739, 0.2048** – Butchershole car park, **50.7759, 0.1521** – Seven Sisters car park) / Friston Forest, Old Willingdon Road, East Dean, Eastbourne, East Sussex, BN20 0AT / *www.forestryengland.uk/friston-forest*

Friston has loads of mountain biking – go exploring or find a local, and be aware of other users. There is authorised off-bridleway horse riding on specific routes for those with a permit, so there may be horses not necessarily where you were expecting them. There are also quite a few bridleways leading through the wood, which can easily be included as part of a longer ride.

Trails

■ Jeremy Cole mountain bike trail – 9 kilometres. This trail can be started from either car park. It is fast and undulating singletrack through the forest and has a very natural feel. It is on chalk so it can get slippery when damp.

Multi-use trails

■ 6.25 kilometres. A family cycle trail.

BETTESHANGER PARK

51.2368, 1.3689 / Sandwich Road, Deal, Kent, CT14 0BF / *www.betteshanger-park.co.uk*

This is a country park with lots of activities, mostly aimed at families rather than mountain bikers. Expect it to be busy in the school holidays. There are also coaching sessions available, giving you the opportunity to improve your skills.

Trails

■ 7 kilometres. This is a winding track through woodland, but then it opens out a bit in the parkland. It can hold water and get muddy. It's nothing very technical, so is great for beginners.
■ 11 kilometres, including the blue. The red sections are extensions to the blue trail. Still, it is nothing overly difficult.

Other features

There is also a 3-kilometre, one-way tarmac cycle track for your inner roadie or for practising safely riding on tarmac.

REDBRIDGE CYCLING CENTRE

51.6060, 0.1282 / Forest Road, Hainault, Redbridge, Essex, IG6 3HP / *visionrcl.org.uk/centre/redbridge-cycling-centre*

This is a good, safe place to advance basic skills. There is lots of coaching available and many adaptive bikes for hire depending on your needs.

Trails

There are several short MTB tracks of varying difficulty here, as well as a road circuit, a pump track and a BMX track. You will need to check the centre's timetable and book in advance.

LEE VALLEY VELOPARK

51.5506, -0.0150 / Abercrombie Road, Queen Elizabeth Olympic Park, London, E20 3AB / *www.visitleevalley.org.uk*

This is part of the 2012 Olympic legacy. The velodrome here is the one used for the 2012 Olympic Games but is also still used for international events. Similarly, the BMX track is the Olympic one. Both have everything between taster and full-on race sessions. There's also a short road circuit. You will need to check the timetable and book in advance.

Trails

There are several short MTB tracks of varying difficulty, and skills sessions are available, but the main focus here is the Olympic tracks.

ASTON HILL BIKE PARK

51.7828, -0.7087 / Aston Hill, Wendover, Buckinghamshire, HP22 5NQ / Trail maintenance: Aston Hill / *www.astonhill.co.uk*

At the time of writing (autumn 2024), Aston Hill is closed following tree felling work. It is scheduled to reopen in 2025.

Most of the trails here are aimed at the gravity lover, as it claims to be a slice of the Alps in the Chiltern Hills. The trails are, necessarily, shorter than those in the Alps due to the size of the hill, but they pack a punch and are well regarded. The place has suffered badly from ash dieback and has needed specialist felling work. This has resulted in closing the trails temporarily while this takes place. Forestry England promise the trails will reopen with new investment.

Trails
Basing this description on what the trails were like before the tree felling and what the current aims are for the rebuild, it's likely there will be an 8-kilometre XC loop suitable for warming up on and for pedalling to the top of the hill. Then several enduro/DH-style tracks increasing in difficulty. Expect lots of off-camber, rooty sections and trails that make the most of the steepness of the land, drops, berms and some interestingly tight corners.

Other features
Also, there's a pump track and a 4X track.

WOBURN SANDS

Under the generic title of Woburn Sands are several areas for riding. Rushmere Country Park has an XC loop and a DH/jump area, and Aspley Woods has XC trails plus the DH/jump section known as Woburn Bike Park. You will need a permit in order to ride on any of the trails.

ASPLEY WOODS

52.0003, -0.6537 / Woburn Sands, Milton Keynes, Buckinghamshire, MK17 8TS / *www.greensandtrust.org/local-site-aspley-woods*

A part of Aspley Woods is the bike park, which is possibly what most people mean by 'Woburn'. You will need a permit for riding on the trails – details on the website.

Trails
Aspley Woods has XC trails plus the DH/jump section known as Woburn Bike Park.
■ **Danesborough, 4 kilometres.** A short singletrack loop through the trees.
■ **Longslade, 9 kilometres.** An XC-style loop, with fairly natural-feeling trails undulating through the woodland. Expect mud in the winter.

WOBURN BIKE PARK

52.0058, -0.6438 / Woburn Road, Milton Keynes, Buckinghamshire, MK17 8TS / Trail maintenance: Woburn Bike Trails Facebook page, including the notorious Kiing of Spades / *www.greensandtrust.org/cycling*

A legendary and epic jump spot which holds annual jams and is ridden by some of the best slopestyle and dirt jumpers in the UK, as well as lesser mortals. There is every sort of dirt jump here you could ever require, and in all sizes. It is a constantly developing area. The trails are sandy and so drain well, and there is lots and lots to session. You will need a permit for riding on the trails – details on the website.

Trails
There are several short enduro/DH runs, again sandy in nature and well-draining, also with jumps of varying sizes.

RUSHMERE COUNTRY PARK

51.9470, -0.6726 / Linslade Road, Heath and Reach, Leighton Buzzard, Bedfordshire, LU7 0EB / *www.greensandtrust.org/cycling*

Remember: you will need a permit for riding on the trails – details on the website.

Trails
■ **Ridge Riders Cross Country Trail, 6 kilometres** with some red sections. As with Aspley Woods, this is fairly natural-feeling singletrack undulating through the woods.
■ **Ridge Riders Downhill Zone.** An area with some bigger drops and jumps to session. It's graded nicely so that it's progressive. There's a full rollable blue trail, a red with harder sections and optional gaps, and then a black with bigger and gnarlier features and unavoidable obstacles.

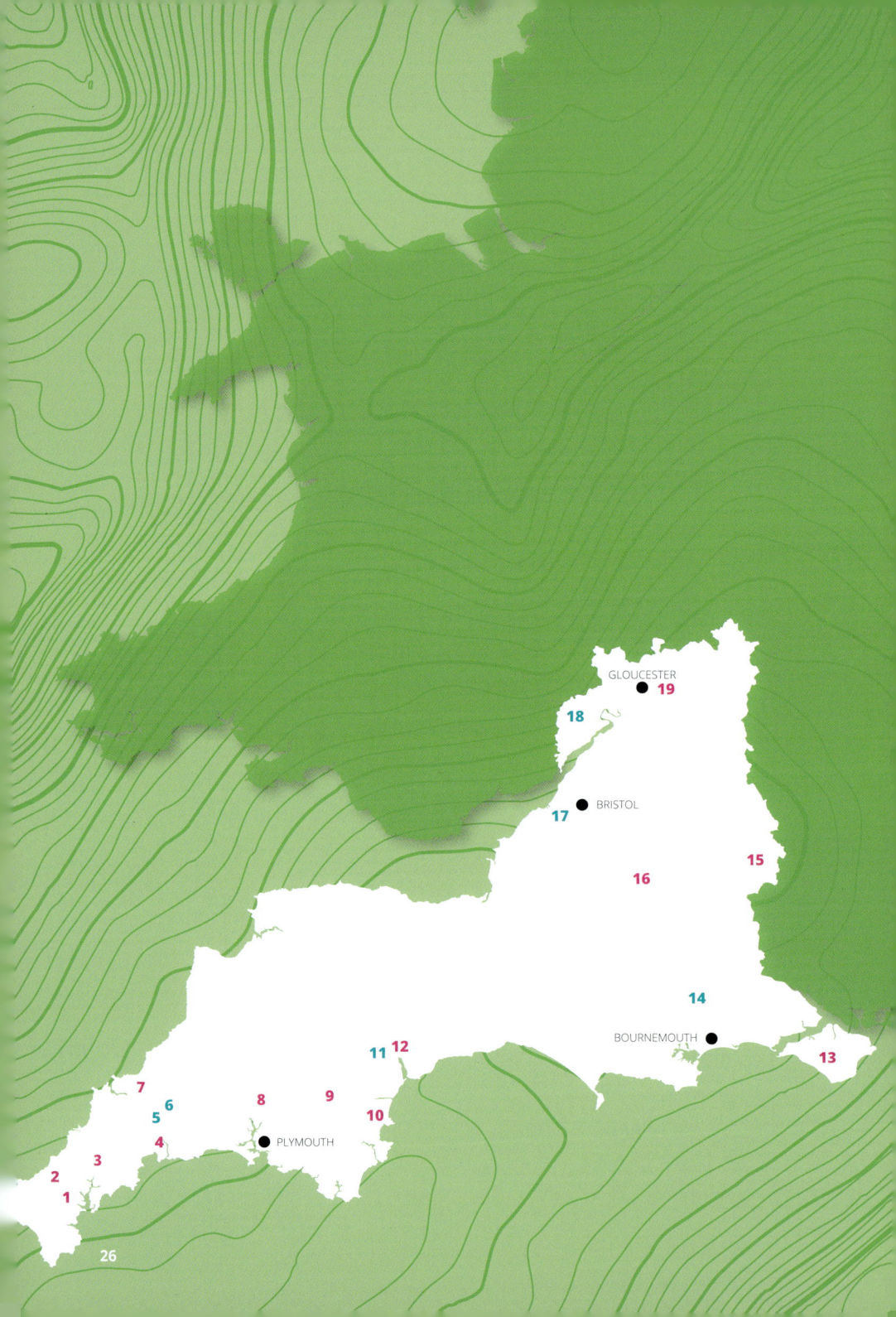

SOUTH WEST ENGLAND

There's a great variety of trail riding in the South West, possibly more than you might at first realise – from gentle pottering through to full-on gnarr; from easy XC to some seriously big jumps. There's also plenty of places where the trail builders have made the absolute most of the steep hillsides.

1. Chacewood Bike Park *p30*
2. The Track *p30*
3. Bike Park Kernow *p30*
4. Woody's Bike Park *p30*
5. Lanhydrock House and Gardens *p31*
6. Cardinham Woods *p32*
7. Old Hill Bike Park *p32*
8. Gawton Gravity Hub *p32*
9. Dartmoor Bike Park *p33*
10. Scadson Freeride Park *p33*
11. Haldon Forest Park *p35*
12. Exeter Bike Park *p35*
13. Isle of Wight Mountain Bike Centre *p35*
14. Moors Valley Country Park and Forest *p36*
15. Tidworth Freeride B1KEPARK *p37*
16. Wind Hill B1KEPARK *p38*
17. Bristol *p38*
18. Forest of Dean Cycle Centre *p40*
19. 417 Bike Park *p41*

SOUTH WEST ENGLAND

OLD HILL BIKE PARK. © *JOOLZE DYMOND*

THE DIRT DIRECTORY

CHACEWOOD BIKE PARK

50.2454, -5.1505 / Wheal Prosper House, Twelveheads, Truro, Cornwall, TR4 8SN / *chacewood.co.uk*

No parking on site – it's a few minutes' ride from the village of Chacewater.

Small but awesome bike park in Cornwall with lots of flow and jump lines. Nicely progressive too with a short walk back up the hill so sessioning is easy. There are blue trails with features that can be sent or rolled as skill levels allow, through to black lines with bigger gap jumps.

You'll need to check when they are open and arrange a pass via their website or Facebook page. The good folk here are also involved with the local grass-roots racing scene, and jump coaching can be arranged on site as well. Armour is probably a good idea; full-face helmets are compulsory for under 16s.

There's also some cracking riding nearby at Poldice Mine and Mars that's well worth checking out, plus the Mineral Trail connecting the north and south coasts of Cornwall is a great mostly off-road easy trail.

THE TRACK

50.2548, -5.2404 / New Portreath Road, Redruth, Cornwall, TR16 4HN / *the-track.co.uk*

Open spring to autumn, weekends with an evening session on Wednesdays, but with additional opening during school holidays. You'll need to book, either online or in person.

Cornish jump park with lots and lots and LOTS of jumps. Plenty of variety in size, from small rollers to huge gaps and everything in between. Fantastic place for progression, and coaching is available. Armour always advised for jumping.

BIKE PARK KERNOW

50.3221, -4.9098 / Trenowth Woods, Grampound Road, Cornwall TR2 4EH / *bikeparkkernow.uk*

Open from spring to autumn, mostly at weekends, but check the website for additional school and bank holiday opening times. Ride passes available as a pre-order or on the day if they have room. Another small but awesome Cornish site constantly being developed. A range of blue to black trails – the blues are flowy with the odd feature that is rollable for the nervous and sendable for the more confident. The reds step the level up a touch but keep things rollable, and obviously expect a little more gnarr from the black. There's a lot of grass-roots enduro racing here too, with the park being very supportive of local riding.

WOODY'S BIKE PARK

50.3461, -4.6693 / Higher Lampetho Farm, Fowey, Cornwall, PL23 1JU / *www.woodysbikepark.com*

A Cornish family owned-and-run bike park. Jon Wood has an amazing collection of retro MTBs – riding is a passion here. The park is seasonal, so check opening times before you travel – their Instagram often has the most up-to-date information: *@woodysbikepark*

You will need a day pass to ride. There is uplift on some days or you can opt to ride up, but it's quite a haul from the bottom of the valley. That being said, it obviously means there's a lot of down to ride too. It's quite an exposed site which can really catch the wind, and on those days jumping is trickier.

The site is in constant development, and again is split between flow/jump and more DH/enduro-style lines (full-face helmets and body armour are compulsory on some trails). It has also been used for the national XC series on several occasions.

SOUTH WEST ENGLAND

WOODY'S BIKE PARK. © *JOOLZE DYMOND*

Trails

There's a mix of trails from blue through to the pro line. As ever, if this is your first time here start on the blues to get the feel of the place. It's also possible to session parts of the tracks, but obviously don't be an idiot and walk back up the trails themselves.

■ **Es Ol.** This is flowy and rollable with plenty of berms and rollers.

■ **Jump line.** A blue jump line which is still flowy and rollable.

■ **Dirt Wave.** The jumps and the berms start to get bigger here, but they are still rollable.

■ **Granite Garden.** This comes off the blue jump line and has several rock garden features. It's made of granite, oddly enough.

■ **Red DH.** An alternative line to Granite Garden, with some drops and techy features.

■ **Twisted Sister.** This is the black jump line, with bigger jumps and berms.

■ **Valley of the Bones.** This is the black DH line, with drop-offs, doubles, rock gardens and so on.

■ **Pro line: Digger.** A huge jump line for those with the skills and nerve to do them. It's definitely not for everyone.

LANHYDROCK HOUSE AND GARDENS

50.4409, -4.6971 / Lanhydrock, Bodmin, Cornwall, PL30 4AB / *www.nationaltrust.org.uk/visit/ cornwall/lanhydrock*

This is more of a destination for families than for hardcore mountain bikers, but the trails can be fun as part of a day out to the house and gardens.

Trails

All of the trails are really designed for family use. Some trails do have some inclines to contend with, which may not suit all, but they are not too technical and the trails do have the benefit of being one way and for cyclists only. There has been no real development of the trails, so they are a little old school.

■ **Bazley's Trail, 3 kilometres.** This is a lovely, gentle introduction to riding off-road with small features. It can be cut short.

■ **Walter's Trail, 1 kilometre.** This is a moderate step up from Bazley's, with slightly larger features, but still nothing too big.

■ **Hart Trail, 1.5 kilometres.** This is a further step up in technicality, and a trail that can be ridden a bit faster. Ends with a fairly chunky (for small legs) climb back up to the house.

■ **Timber Trail, 1.5 kilometres.** The site's most technical trail – although that's by National Trust standards – with steeper gradients and more corners. Also ends with the fairly chunky climb back up to the house.

■ **The Saw Pit, 500 metres.** This is a dual slalom track. It's short and slightly trickier than the blue trails, but still nothing too technical.

■ **Skills trail.** This is small and usually busy.

Multi-use trails

■ **Lodge Trail, 2.5 kilometres.**

THE DIRT DIRECTORY

CARDINHAM WOODS. © *JOOLZE DYMOND*

CARDINHAM WOODS

50.4697, -4.6784 / Bodmin, Cornwall, PL30 4AL / www.forestryengland.uk/cardinham-woods

There is only really one biking trail here, but there are walking trails including one to a disused silver and lead mine.

Trails

■ **Bodmin Beast, 12 kilometres.** This is a really thoughtfully designed blue trail: climbs are graded and switchbacked, leading to fun downhills – if you aren't good at corners these won't be your favourite features. It's well built enough that it's suitable for beginners, but is also a lot of fun at speed for the more advanced rider. It's what blue trails should aspire to be like. The climbing does get to feel quite cumulative, though, but there are ways of using fire roads to get back to the start if it all becomes too much.

■ **Hell's Teeth and Dialled-In-Dave** add a couple of kilometres, but not much more in terms of technicality.

OLD HILL BIKE PARK

50.5353, -4.7800 / Bodmin, Cornwall, PL30 3EF / oldhillbikepark.co.uk

An incredibly friendly, laid-back place to ride. It's family owned and run, plus they can give you pointers on where to buy the best pasties locally. There is a burger van at weekends and the park is open until dusk, so summer shredding lasts until late in the day.

You will need a day pass to ride, which can be booked online beforehand, and you will need to sign a waiver before riding. All the trails involve a push up to the top, although there is plenty of room between trails to cut across and session.

Trails

Imagine a sloping field full of tracks with jumps of varying size which are continually being developed and improved – that's pretty much Old Hill. There are flow and jump lines of every size and every grade, and the blues and reds are all rollable if you prefer, so they are perfect for learning and progressing. The black trails have unavoidable gaps and jumps, so make sure you know what you are expecting. There's also lots of trickable jumps; the freerider Tom Isted lives fairly locally and rides here – that's how good the jumps are.

All the tracks are well built and maintained, and they are suitable for all ages and abilities. This is a superb hidden gem.

GAWTON GRAVITY HUB

50.5066, -4.1750 / B3257, Tavistock, Devon, PL19 8JN / *gawtongravityhub.com*

Gawton Gravity Hub is very much geared to DH/enduro/techy-style trails, but also has some big jumps. Protection and a full-face helmet are advisable. This is not a place for the unconfident; there is no real beginner stuff here, but **HSD** is rollable and suitable for building skills which you can take to the other tracks. There is lots of stuff of all sizes to session, and

SOUTH WEST ENGLAND

OLD HILL BIKE PARK. © JOOLZE DYMOND

work is constantly ongoing to maintain and improve trails on the site. It's a great place to improve your techy skills.

You will need membership or a day pass to ride. For all the trails you will need to ride or push back up to the top.

Trails
The trails here range from red through to double black. These are not trail centre grades, so the red-graded **HSD** flow trail is the one to start on to get the feel of the place. All of the HSD trail is rollable, but there's plenty of stuff to jump if you prefer. After this, the trails start to get more serious, with some drops and gaps; you should be able to find something to scare yourself on. Look carefully at the trail gradings before over-committing to something new, and always have a look at new features before sending them. There's a lot of quite natural-feeling DH trails and there are plenty of local races run here.

Rattler is a short but big jump line, with unavoidable gaps which can easily be sessioned.

DARTMOOR BIKE PARK

50.5172, -3.7890 / River Dart Country Park, Ashburton, Devon, TQ13 7NP / *riverdart. co.uk/family-park-attractions/ dartmoor-bike-park-2*

This is a tiny bike park attached to a campsite and family adventure attraction on the edge of Dartmoor. It's somewhere you'd ride as part of a visit to the country park. You will need a day pass to ride, in addition to the park entry.

Trails
Four short runs of blue, red, black and orange grades, with the emphasis on jumps.

SCADSON FREERIDE PARK

50.4592, -3.5712 / Scadson Woods, Cockington Road, Paignton, Devon, TQ3 1RW / *scadsonfreeride.com*

There has been riding in Scadson Woods for a very long time, but now there are properly built and maintained trails with a DH/enduro feel, plus a freeride line with very big jumps. This is not really a place for beginners: you will get more out of it if you are reasonably confident with your wheels off the ground. The trails aren't surfaced, so they change with the weather conditions.

You will need a membership or a day pass to ride. All the trails are push up, and armour and a full-face helmet are recommended for the bigger trails. There's no on-site parking, so you will need to ride in.

Trails
You need to be a reasonably confident rider to get the best out of the trails. There are a couple of starting points, so make sure you get the right one. The trails can be quite tightly packed in on the hillside, so steady away until you know where you are going.

■ **Training Wheels.** This is the easiest of the trails, so it's best to start with this one so you can get a feel of the place and the terrain. It's nominally blue, but that's bike park not trail centre grading – there are drops and features and it can get quite techy, especially in the wet.

The other trails then increase in difficulty and the size of features, but it's easy to session stuff and progress your riding. Expect steep tech, drops and gaps galore.

■ **Black Pig.** This pro line is a line of large doubles, berms and hips, with the jumps being of a trickable size, so make sure you know what you are doing before you send them.

Other features
There's also a skills area with jumps and drops near the top of the park.

SOUTH WEST ENGLAND

HALDON FOREST PARK

50.6518, -3.5798 / Bullers Hill, Kennford, Devon, EX6 7XR / *www.forestryengland.uk/haldon-forest-park*

This is a great place for beginners and families. There are plenty of trails to progress on, from starting to ride off-road to trying a reasonably easy red. Plus, there are running and walking routes in the forest if you are with others who don't want to ride or fancy a change of scenery.

Trails

🟦 **Spicers Trail, 3.7 kilometres.** There are no steep gradients on this trail and there's nothing technical, but it is perfect for those starting out in off-roading and is short enough to do laps. It's one way and off-road which is unusual – and great – for a trail like this.

🟦 **Kiddens Trail, 6.4 kilometres.** This is the more technical blue trail, with a couple of slightly tricky bits for the unwary. There's a lot more up and down than Spicers Trail, and correspondingly a lot more fun to be had. It's great for both the less confident rider and those who have more experience.

🟧 **Ridge Ride Trail, 9.6 kilometres.** This is at the easier end of the red scale of things, with a few technical sections, but it is at a good level for those building up to red. There's lots of singletrack with only one fire road climb – nice and flowy. You can also ride sections of it as a taster with careful reading of the trail map.

⬛ **Ridge Ride Extreme, 900 metres.** This is an additional section to the red route. It starts with a rock garden as a qualifier and then has roots, berms and more rocks with a super-smooth flow section in the middle. It can get sloppy. There's a fire road climb back to the start.

Multi-use trails

🟩 Discovery Trail, 2.5 kilometres.

Other features

🟧 Pump track and skills area. These are small but fun.

EXETER BIKE PARK

50.6753, -3.5228 / Pottles Farm, Days Pottles Lane, Exeter, Devon, EX6 8BB / *www.exeterbikepark.co.uk*

All the trails here involve a push up to the top. The emphasis is on flow and jumps, and because the park was designed by pro rider Kye Forte, that's exactly what you get; if you aren't confident with your wheels off the ground, this place isn't going to be for you. It's on a hillside so it can catch the wind, which may affect your stability in the air. You will need a day pass to ride, and protection and full-face helmets are recommended.

Trails

🟦 Lots of jumps and rollers, and all are rollable.

🟧 The jumps are a lot bigger than the blue trail, but still are all rollable.

⬛ The jumps are even bigger, with unavoidable gaps.

Each level of jump is marked with coloured posts so there are no nasty surprises.

ISLE OF WIGHT MOUNTAIN BIKE CENTRE

50.6574, -1.3523 / Cheverton Farm, Shorwell, Isle of Wight, PO30 3JE / *www.isleofwightmountainbikecentre.com*

Brainchild and home farm of Sam Hodgson, the freerider who also has his training compound here, this is a centre which is continually developing and aims to be able to provide something for the majority of riders. It also has the only purpose-built MTB trails on the Isle of Wight.

You will need to book. The centre is seasonal, so check opening times and what developments there have been recently. The centre's aim is to provide a kind of hybrid approach to trail centres, allowing you to mix and match trails according to your mood or skill level, so it's easy to try a bit of this and that, which

THE DIRT DIRECTORY

GAWTON GRAVITY HUB. © *JOOLZE DYMOND*

all helps with progression. Skills sessions are also available, although they may not leave you being able to ride like Sam Hodgson.

Well used by locals and their families, this is a real asset, catering for many styles of riding in a really fun way.

Trails

There are plenty of trails of all levels, including a 3.5-kilometre green loop aimed at families and beginners. There are flowy trails, techy trails and, as you might expect, plenty of chances to get your wheels off the ground. Some trails are surfaced and weatherproof, others more natural, meaning they will change with the weather. There are also some really fun bits of woodwork to add a bit of spice to the riding.

MOORS VALLEY COUNTRY PARK AND FOREST

50.8505, -1.8497 / Horton Road, Ashley Heath, Dorset, BH24 2ET / www.moors-valley.co.uk/activity/cycling-trails

   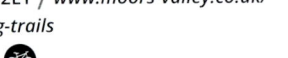

There are lots of tracks within this country park on which cycling is permitted alongside the waymarked trails, plus lots of other things to do such as playgrounds, walking trails, a narrow-gauge railway and other activities in school holidays and weekends. It therefore easily makes for a good family day out. However, be aware of other users in the forest.

Trails

■ **Through the Forest, 7 kilometres.** This is the park's dedicated MTB trail. It comprises pleasant singletrack through the trees without anything too technical. It does include some boardwalk, but it is wide.

■ **Watchmoor Bike Park**, located within the county park, has several short singletrack runs, some drops and dirt jumps, and a pump track. It's great for sessioning and pushing your riding. The closest parking for access to the bike park is at Watchmoor car park (**50.8477, -1.8105**).

Multi-use trails

■ **Corsican Circuit, 3.2 kilometres.** This has additional extras up to 10 kilometres on mostly gravel paths and roads.

SOUTH WEST ENGLAND

GAWTON GRAVITY HUB. © *JOOLZE DYMOND*

TIDWORTH FREERIDE B1KEPARK

51.2192, -1.6650 / A338, Tidworth, Wiltshire, SP9 7TE / *www.b1ke.com/b1keparks/tidworth-freeride*

Tidworth was built originally by the local DH and jump crews but is now part of the B1KEPARK group and offers a mix of DH/enduro-style tracks and freeride.

You will need either membership or a day pass to ride. For regulars to this park or to all of the B1KEPARKS there are good value annual membership options. Full-face helmets and armour are recommended for the gnarlier stuff. All the trails require a push up.

The trail grading here involves both the colour of trail and a lozenge/dot system to give you further information: a single lozenge means it's a gentler trail and everything can be rolled; two-lozenge trails have bigger features and stuff that it's better not to roll, although alternative lines may be available; three lozenges mean you need to be comfortable and competent with your wheels off the ground. Both the colour grading and lozenge number should give you a reasonable amount of information about the trail, but as always with this kind of place, it's worth having a good look at features before riding them. There is also plenty of information about the trails on the website.

Trails

Tidworth had a huge rebuild in 2024 and is quite different to the previous offering. There's still a mix of jump and DH lines, but more emphasis on jump and flow now. Bear in mind that as the place is on chalk there are great differences in riding conditions between wet and dry weather – it can be rather greasy in certain conditions. **Waspy** is a great place to start with a little bit of everything, serving as a warm-up for the gnarlier trails and will be an indicator of how the place will suit you. There's several red flowy jumpy trails that can be mixed and matched to give variation – **White Line (Top)**, **Berminator**, **Berminator Too** and **Oblivion** can all be ridden. White Line also continues to the bottom of the park but gets more serious on the lower part with unavoidable and non-rollable gaps. **Peaky Blind-Hits** and **Peaks & Troughs** supply bigger jumps. For those wanting a bit of tech then there's **River Flow** and **Hooper Struve**.

Other features

There's also a jump progression area, **Humps 'n' Bumps**, with a range of sizes of jumps, ideal for warming up or honing skills.

WIND HILL B1KEPARK

51.1859, -2.2425 / The Red Way, Warminster, Wiltshire, BA12 7NW / *www.b1ke.com/b1keparks/wind-hill*

Despite all the pro videos shot here, there is stuff for lesser mortals to ride too and plenty of opportunity for progression. Tracks are constantly being tweaked and maintained, so there is nearly always something fresh.

You will need either a membership or a day pass to ride, and frequent visitors can take advantage of better-value annual memberships. Full-face helmets and armour are recommended for the techier stuff.

The trail grading uses the colour of trail and a lozenge/dot system: a single lozenge means it's a gentler trail and everything can be rolled; two-lozenge trails have bigger features and features that it's better not to roll, although alternative lines may be available; three lozenges mean you need to be comfortable and competent with your wheels off the ground. This combined grading system should give you a reasonable amount of detail, but as always it's sometimes worth having a good look at features before committing to riding them. There is plenty of information on the park's website about the trails. All the trails require a push up.

Trails

Pay attention to the trail map to check you are on the right trail, as they mostly all come off the same blue top track. For Bluetopia, keep right along that top track.

Freeride – the flowier, jumpier trails:
- **Bluetopia.** This is the classic starting point, either as a way to get a feel for the park or as a warm-up. It's flowy and has rollers and berms, and you can start to hone your jumping skills here. It's a brilliant track for all levels of riding.
- **Empuru.** This is a jump trail and includes split-sided jumps (shorter on one side than the other) to aid progression. There are lots of flowy berms too.
- **Pay Rise.** Flowy, bermy and jumpy with some lines which will need a fair commitment, others that have alternative lines.
- **The Step Up.** A stand-alone feature ideal for sessioning. As the name suggests it's a big step-up. Just watch for the tree on landing.
- **Viagra Falls.** This is the pro line, with huge trickable jumps. It is only for the very capable and confident. If that's not you, you can watch others having a go.

DH – the nadgier, techier side:
- **Tina Turner.** Plenty of corners and roots. Sometimes together.
- **The Left Hand Side.** An easier version of Pass the Dutchie.
- **Feed 'em to the Lions.** Lots of line choices, and sessioning will not only help you to get the best out of the trail but also help your skills progress as most features can be rolled before you get to the sending stage.
- **Rootiful South.** As the name suggests there's one or two roots along the way, plus some steep sections with added roots.
- **Ark at Ee.** This DH trail is technical at the top but more flowy with some big jumps at the bottom; it does have some unavoidable gaps.
- **Pass the Dutchie.** This has plenty of line choices, so it will take some sessioning to get right. It's technical and natural.

BRISTOL

A short distance from Bristol city centre are several woods with short, purpose-built trails which can easily be joined together to give a longer ride. Plus, there are lots of bridleways, National Cycle Network routes and other trails locally. Bristol is not short of riding, and local bike shops have plenty of knowledge on the subject. One of the founders of BW Cycling in Bristol is ex-Olympian Oli Beckingsale, who knows a thing or two about riding. Head to *ridebristol.org* for more information.

SOUTH WEST ENGLAND

ASHTON COURT. © *DAVE PRICE/PEDAL PROGRESSION*

ASHTON COURT

51.4513, -2.6439 / Long Ashton, Bristol, BS8 3PX / www.bristol.gov.uk/museums-parks-sports-culture/mountain-biking-at-ashton-court-estate / www.pedalprogression.com

The trails in the grounds of this mansion and country park are a great local resource.

Trails
■ **Nova Cycle Trail, 6.5 kilometres.** This is a well-built, fun and flowy trail with berms and rollers; it's a really good example of a blue trail. There are a few red options along the way as well. The trail has a hard-packed surface so holds up well in most weather.
■ **Super Nova**, an 800-metre option off the main Nova trail. This adds in a bit more technicality, with rollers, berms, rock gardens and drops.

FIFTY ACRE WOOD

51.4544, -2.6660 / Manor Road, Bristol, BS8 3RR / visitbristol.co.uk/things-to-do/mountainbike-trail-50-acre-wood-p1900783

From Ashton Court, cross the road and follow the bridleway up the hill to access the trail. This can also be accessed from the Nova trail at Ashton Court.

Trails
■ **5 kilometres.** This has a natural feel to it, so expect rocks and roots. Grip on this trail will be affected by the weather. It also has some occasional optional red features.

LEIGH WOODS

51.4629, -2.6453 / Abbots Leigh, Bristol, BS8 3QB / www.forestryengland.uk/leigh-woods/yer-tiz-trail-leigh-woods

This can also be accessed from the Ashton Court trails.

Trails
■ **Yer Tiz, 3.6 kilometres.** Fairly natural-feeling singletrack with some red features coming off the main trail every so often. The trail can hold water and get a bit slippery.
■ **Jump line.** A short series of progressive tabletops near the car park.

THE DIRT DIRECTORY

FOREST OF DEAN CYCLE CENTRE. © *MAN DOWN MEDIA*

FOREST OF DEAN CYCLE CENTRE

51.8096, -2.5699 / Cannop Ponds, West Dean, Lydney, Gloucestershire, GL16 7EH /
www.fodmtb.com / Trail maintenance: *www.deantrailvolunteers.org.uk* / Uplift: *www.flyupdownhill.co.uk*

The great thing about the Forest of Dean is that there's plenty of choice for most styles of riding. It's also a good place to be able to push yourself a little because of that variety. There's also coaching and guided rides available for the more advanced rider if you need help with that push. There's fairly regular DH and enduro racing here, and the forest is used for regional XC. It's a popular riding spot, and no wonder.

The Forest of Dean itself is much bigger than just the stuff around Cannop, and has a wealth of history that can be explored. There are loads of tracks and bridleways crossing the area and which link up with trails in the Wye Valley. There is so much riding here of any sort you fancy.

Trails

■ **Old Bob's, 2 kilometres.** A short, wider surfaced trail making it suitable for all bikes – adaptive, balance, tag-a-longs, anything you've got. There are also three skills areas along the way to session if you fancy building up your skills for the blue.

■ **Verderers Trail, 11 kilometres.** A flowy blue trail with a couple of interesting features to spice it up. A great example of a blue trail – it's won awards, and rightly so. An undulating climb is followed by a (mostly) great downhill all the way back to the start.

■ **Freeminers Trail, 6.1–17.3 kilometres.** A little bit of everything with three variants of the trail – 6.1km, 11.3km and 17.3km – depending what you fancy: ups and downs, tight twisty bits and flow but not too many technical features. There is a fair amount of climbing, but, of course, that means downhill sections. All circle back round to the visitor centre.

■ **The downhill tracks** are a 750-metre, or 10–15 minute, walk/ride up, or uplift is available; alternatively you can use the Verderers Trail to ride up in a slower but more pleasant way. There are several tracks to choose from, with something to suit most styles: there's flowy trails, jumpy stuff and natural rooty goodness. Lots of fast fun.

Multi-use trails

■ **Family Trail, 8-kilometre or 14.5-kilometre options.** This is all on surfaced paths but includes optional 'fun zones' along the way, which are slightly more technical sections to play about on.

Other features

There is also a pump track and skills area not far from the centre.

SOUTH WEST ENGLAND

FOREST OF DEAN CYCLE CENTRE. © *MAN DOWN MEDIA*

417 BIKE PARK

51.8397, -2.1148 / Crickley Hill, Witcombe, Gloucestershire, GL3 4UF / *417bikepark.co.uk*

This is a pretty large site, so has room to cater for several different styles of riding, and there are plenty of opportunities to progress your riding. Some tracks are seasonal, so check before you travel.

You will need to register and sign on to ride, but there's also an annual membership for regulars. Full-face helmets are advised on the toughest trails. You can either buy uplift or choose to ride up. There's also coaching available for everything from getting kids off stabilisers to full-on DH training. If 417 Bike Park offers a sort of riding, it offers coaching for it as well.

As usual at this kind of park, stuff is constantly being tweaked, so check the website for the latest news.

Trails

Although these are called DH trails, there are plenty of easier options. You'll need to be a reasonably confident rider rather than an absolute beginner, but there are blue-graded trails which are flowy with rollable features. There's a whole series of red trails with a mix of techier stuff and flowier stuff – check the park's descriptions of the current trails. The reds have rollable or avoidable features, so progression is possible.

For the more advanced riders, there are black and double-black trails. Expect much bigger and scarier features, with unavoidable gaps. A sighting lap is recommended on your first run.

The 4X track is used as a venue for the British National Series, but is rollable for beginners and sendable for experts.

Dual slalom track – for the settling of arguments between friends about who is faster.

There's even a trail to the uplift.

Other features

There's a dirt jump field with a range of sizes of jumps. There is a beginner line with tables, the main line with doubles, shark fins and hips, and the pro line with a set of large, trickable doubles; plenty of stuff on which to progress.

THE MIDLANDS & EAST ANGLIA

The Midlands and East Anglia are not the hilliest parts of the country, so gravity-based tracks aren't so much of a thing here, but there's some great XC and some amazing jump spots where trail builders have used the land to make the most of the smaller hills. These areas can get busy, too: both Sherwood Pines and Cannock Chase Forest get a lot of visitors. Ride at Tunstall Forest, though, and you could well have the place to yourself.

1. Hopton Wood *p46*
2. Eastridge Woods *p46*
3. Burlish Bike Park *p48*
4. Sandwell Valley Country Park *p48*
5. Cannock Chase Forest *p48*
6. Stile Cop Downhill Trails *p49*
7. Glapwell *p50*
8. Sherwood Pines *p50*
9. Northampton Bike Park *p52*
10. Chicksands Bike Park *p52*
11. Ingrebourne Hill *p53*
12. Hadleigh Country Park *p55*
13. Phoenix Bike Park *p55*
14. Thetford Forest – High Lodge *p56*
15. Twisted Oaks Bike Park and Trails *p56*
16. Tunstall Forest *p57*
17. Skillz Bike Park *p58*

SHERWOOD PINES. © *JOHN COEFIELD*

THE DIRT DIRECTORY

HOPTON WOOD

52.3945, -2.9577 / Hopton Wood, Craven Arms, Shropshire, SY7 0QF / *www.forestryengland.uk/hopton-wood* / Uplift: *www.pearcecycles.co.uk*

Hopton Wood is another place that's been used for lots of racing over the years, and still is. The local Pearce Cycles have a close relationship with the place and organise racing and occasional uplift. The trails certainly make the most of the terrain: there's a lot of choice for riding in a relatively small place. Hopton can be ridden by riders of all abilities and yet still be challenging in places for many, too.

Trails

■ **Warm-up loop, 1 kilometre.** This winds through the trees to give you a taste of the place. It could be used as an introductory trail as well.

■ **Qualifier, 1.7 kilometres.** This comes off the blue warm-up trail. The idea is that if you are happy on this, you'll be happy with the longer red trail.

■ **Pearce XC, 12.6 kilometres.** A fairly natural-feeling trail, so expect it to change under tyre when it's wet. A lot of climbing is involved, but much of that is done on thoughtfully constructed singletrack – this also means there's a lot of fun downhill singletrack too. There are plenty of places where you can cut the trail short if you need to, and the way back to the car park is regularly signed. A nice and varied trail.

■ **Three DH/enduro trails.** These are still used for DH racing, but are not particularly extreme. Most of the features can be rolled or avoided, although that's not really the point. Good for challenging yourself, with a nice mix of rooty goodness and some steeper sections with drops and jumps.

Multi-use trails

■ **Hopton Blue, 4 kilometres.** Wide tracks, and no longer waymarked.

EASTRIDGE WOODS

52.6189, -2.8996 / Eastridge Woods, Habberley, Shrewsbury, Shropshire, SY5 0TP / *www.forestryengland.uk/eastridge-woods* / Trail maintenance: *www.facebook.com/groups/eastridgetrailpartnership*

Eastridge Woods is one of the oldest MTB sites in the UK, with a lengthy DH pedigree. It still hosts enduro and XC races. The site has a natural feel, so expect roots and mud rather than groomed trails, and there are lots of purpose-built features. There are many trails in the woods, but local knowledge is really needed in order to get the best out of it, or very careful reading of Trailforks. It can be quite a brutal place on a hardtail!

EASTRIDGE WOODS. © *JOOLZE DYMOND*

Trails

■ **Revelation Trail, 8.4 kilometres.** This is very techy in places for a red trail; it's not your average XC course. Also, it tends to be badly waymarked and if you come off route you may end up on something way out of your comfort zone. It's not for those just moving up to red trails. However, if you like unmanicured, technical trails there's some great riding: there's rocks, roots and more steepness than usually encountered on a red trail.

■ **Three DH/enduro trails.** Expect steep and techy trails – they're more technical than a lot of Forestry England black trails. They're excellent for those who like steep and gnarly natural trails and are great for getting your enduro bro on; they're to be avoided if that makes you shudder. It's probably wise to wear some armour.

THE DIRT DIRECTORY

CANNOCK CHASE FOREST. © *JOHN COEFIELD*

BURLISH BIKE PARK

52.3568, -2.2884 / Kingsway, Stourport-on-Severn, Worcestershire, DY13 8NJ / *burlishbikepark.com*

Burlish has been an unofficial jump spot for decades but is now official thereby protecting its future. You'll need to sign a waiver and buy a pass to ride – the money goes back into maintaining the trails so it's well worth it. While predominantly focused on jumps, there's also a family/all-access green trail around the outside of the park, and a blue dual slalom track for racing your mates which is suitable for most riders. Then the jump lines start with a series of blue tables and work their way up to red and black gaps. Full-face helmets and armour recommended on the jump lines. Lots of jumps, lots of fun.

SANDWELL VALLEY COUNTRY PARK

52.5278, -1.9625 / Park Lane, West Bromwich, West Midlands, B71 3SZ / *www.sandwellvalley.com/cycling*

North-east of Birmingham is this free-to-use bike park (a trail centre, really) with trails for all abilities, from green through to (easy) black. There's the 3-kilometre blue (with red and black options) Miners' Trail on one side of the road, and Hilltop Bike Park on the other; the downhill trails here are fairly short and feature the usual jumps and berms. Worth a visit if you're in the area or don't need to travel far.

CANNOCK CHASE FOREST

52.7513, -1.9729 / Birches Valley, Rugeley, Staffordshire, WS15 2UQ / *www.forestryengland.uk/cannock-chase-forest* / Trail maintenance: *www.chasetrails.co.uk*

Cannock Chase is very popular, both with riders and other users. There are plenty of off-piste trails across the Chase as well as the way-marked trails. It was also the host site for the Commonwealth Games XC in 2022, although the more exciting features of that course were removed after the games so that people wouldn't hurt themselves on large features. It's also popular for local XC events and regularly hosts a round of the National XC series.

It can get soggy in winter and after wet weather.

Be very careful of your bike in the main visitor car park – sadly, it's an absolute hotspot for bike theft.

Trails

🟦 **Perry's Trail, 4.3 kilometres.** A trail suitable for novices and families. A smooth, surfaced trail with rollable features and berms, and a couple of optional red features. It's not too hilly, so is good for little legs too. This is the blue trail Cannock has needed for years.

🟥 **Follow the Dog, 10.8 kilometres.** This is the original Cannock trail, sort of: it has been revised and developed significantly since first opening. It gets a lot of use and so is vulnerable to wear. The trail features are either rollable or an alternative is given – however, be aware of the Cannock pebbles, which are rounded and interesting to ride on, especially in the wet.

THE MIDLANDS & EAST ANGLIA

CANNOCK CHASE FOREST. © *JOHN COEFIELD*

■ **The Monkey, 22.8 kilometres** (including Follow the Dog). This is a considerable extension to Follow The Dog, including much more ascent and many more trail features. Overall, it's quite a bit more challenging than Follow the Dog. There are several black features for a bit of extra spiciness; all join back into the main red trail.

Multi-use trails
■ Fairoak Trail, 4 kilometres.
■ Pedal and Play Trail, 2 kilometres.
Designed with British Cycling to help kids develop their off-road skills.

STILE COP DOWNHILL TRAILS

52.7342, -1.9490 / **Stile Cop Road, Rugeley, Staffordshire, WS15 1QR (not precise, but the car park is on Google Maps)** / **Trail maintenance:** *stilecop.com*

A stone's throw from the main Cannock trails, Stile Cop is a relatively short hill, but the tracks make the most of the available drop – full-face helmets and armour are recommended. Racers Guild Racing hold DH events here – search out their Facebook page for updates.

Stile Cop can get soggy in winter and after wet weather. Expect greasy roots in the damp. Plus, watch out for the notoriously slippery Cannock pebbles in places.

It's possible to ride across from the main Cannock Chase trails to Stile Cop.

Trails
There is very much a DH/enduro slant to all of the trails – this is not XC riding. All the trails here are classed as red, black or orange, with one, two or three skulls refining the difficulty distinction further. They are waymarked at the top from the two starting points, but these are not always the easiest trails to follow once you are on them, as several of the blacks come off the red. Ease of wayfinding can depend on how recently the signs have been updated.

The easiest trails, though, are fairly straightforward if you've managed to stay on the right track. Then there are harder trails with gaps and drops. There are chicken runs around most features, but that's not playing the game.

The vertical drop of the hill is 65 metres, which means the runs aren't overly long, but they are good quality and make the most of that drop. It will definitely feel like more than 65 metres on the push back to the top!

This is very much a place to session.

THE DIRT DIRECTORY

GLAPWELL. © *JOHN COEFIELD*

SHERWOOD PINES. © *JOHN COEFIELD*

GLAPWELL

53.1922, -1.3019 / Stockley Lane, Chesterfield, Derbyshire, S44 5GA / *www.derbyshire.gov.uk/ leisure/countryside/countryside-sites/wildlife-amenity/glapwell-countryside-site.aspx*

Two kilometres of bike-specific and enjoyable blue singletrack plus shared trails on an old colliery site. Nearby, on the other side of the M1, are more shared trails on more old mine workings. Pleasant way to explore the area.

SHERWOOD PINES

53.1671, -1.0861 / Kings Clipstone, Nottingham, Nottinghamshire, NG21 9JL / *www.forestryengland. uk/sherwood-pines*

Sherwood Pines is another very popular Midlands destination, so it can suffer from wear and can get busy with other users. It can also get soggy in winter and after wet weather. Sherwood Pines is pretty flat, so the intensity will come from your speed – and pedalling – rather than the trail, but it has frequently been used as an XC venue for both local and national-level races. Dig days are occasionally run by Forestry England.

Trails

■ **Robin Hood Adventure Trail, 11.2 kilometres.** This is a mix of fire road and blue singletrack, so it's a good introduction to off-roading. The singletrack sections are a mix of old and new, so you'll find some sections are far more fast flowing and have more features than others. Everything is rollable – as it should be on a blue – and it does share some wider singletrack and fire road sections with the green trail. As it's pretty flat, there is a lot of pedalling, so it will make you fitter.

■ **Outlaw Trail, 13 kilometres.** An excellent introductory red XC-style trail, with enough features to keep things interesting for the more advanced. The trail is undulating rather than hilly, and there are no features that can't be rolled or avoided.

Multi-use trails

■ Maid Marion Family Cycle Route, 6.4 kilometres.

Other features

■ **Bike Park.** This can be reached from the red trail and has a jump zone and a downhill zone:

Jump zone. This has several lines of jumps, increasing in difficulty. It's a good area for progressing your jumping skills.

Downhill zone. Comprises several lines with a variety of features such as rock gardens and drop-offs. It starts with a tower to help give you a bit of speed, although this can be avoided if it's too daunting. Don't be intimidated by the DH label – it's more red/black and there is nothing massively big. This section is designed for sessioning.

Skills loop and training area. A small area near the visitor centre.

OPPOSITE SHERWOOD PINES. © *JOOLZE DYMOND*

THE DIRT DIRECTORY

NORTHAMPTON BIKE PARK. © *NORTHAMPTON BIKE PARK*

NORTHAMPTON BIKE PARK

52.2197, -0.8832 / Eagle Drive, Northampton, Northamptonshire, NN4 7DU / *northamptonbikepark.org*

Northampton Bike Park is a former golf course transformed into a centre aimed at having a little bit of something for most riders. It only opened as recently as autumn 2022 and has already become a really useful resource for locals and families.

Trails

The site is split between the easier eastern side and the harder western, and everything is aimed at building confidence and progression.

🟩 As well as a multi-use path, there is a green climb leading to a green-graded flow descent. The idea is that once you are comfy on the green you can try the blue.

🟦 On the eastern side there are a couple of blue descents, again of a flow nature: **PDQ** and **Uncle Fester**. They are short and perfect for building confidence. There is also a blue-graded dual slalom track.

On the western side of the park there are the jumpier lines with a harder rating – again, the idea is once you are happy on the blue you progress to the red and the black. So, the blue starts with rollers and berms, and then things get progressively bigger.

Other features

There's also a skills area.

CHICKSANDS BIKE PARK

52.0616, -0.3740 / Northwood End Road, Shefford, Bedfordshire, SG17 5QQ / www.chicksandsbikepark.co.uk

You will either need to buy a day pass or book in advance to ride at Chicksands. Body armour and a full-face helmet are advised, depending on what you are riding. Coaching is available on site. It is very popular so does get busy, especially at weekends.

There are a whole variety of tracks here, all on the gravity side, with a shortish walk/ride back up. Like most bike parks, trails change and develop on a regular basis. It's not all the gnarly stuff frequently seen on the internet; there is plenty of straightforward stuff here too. It's a great place for progressing your skills: there are areas such as the jump lines where different feature sizes are next to each other, so you can easily measure whether you are ready for the next level.

THE MIDLANDS & EAST ANGLIA

HADLEIGH COUNTRY PARK. © *JOOLZE DYMOND*

Trails

🟢 These are the easiest tracks at Chicksands, especially designed for the smaller rider so they don't get squashed by bigger riders. There's a mini BMX track, a small trail and a couple of pump tracks – all very short, all great fun.

🟦 **The Dual Slalom Track** is recommended as a starting point to get the hang of the terrain. Also, this is a great place to settle arguments between friends. Then there are some blue flow and singletrack lines – these are bike park blues, not trail centres blues, so don't write them off as too easy. Mostly, they are pretty flowy with some smaller, rollable features. Then there's some progression lines which are exactly that: you can work on a particular feature on a short track and progress; for a start, there are drops-off and tables.

🟥 **Lockdown Line and Mini DH.** These trails are where the features start to get bigger and include gaps. It's probably best to check before you ride which can be rolled or avoided and which have to be sent. Then there's the red versions of the progression lines – bigger drops and bigger jumps. And a mulch jump.

⬛ **Snake Run** and **Bull Run.** These are the bigger DH/enduro lines, with big gaps and big features. Check them before riding. In the progression lines there's an even bigger drop-off to practise, and some fair-sized trick jumps. The competition lines are not only used by some of the best dirt jumpers in the country, but for regular comps too.

Other features

There is also a 4X course of national standard, but everything is actually rollable.

INGREBOURNE HILL

51.5259, 0.1935 / Rainham Road, Rainham, Essex, RM13 8ST / www.forestryengland.uk/ingrebourne-hill

Ingrebourne Hill is a small country park with a variety of trails for walkers, horse riders and cyclists. It's a handy local resource, but not one to travel to.

Trails

🟦 **2 kilometres.** A very short but pleasant singletrack – watch out for walkers.

Other features

There is also a pump track and 3 kilometres of multi-use tracks.

HADLEIGH COUNTRY PARK

51.5503, 0.5958 / Chapel Lane, Hadleigh, Benfleet, Essex, SS7 2PP / *www.explore-essex.com/places-to-go/find-whats-near-me/hadleigh-country-park*

This is the legacy track from the 2012 Olympic Games, which sounds a lot more exciting than it is. It's also a constant source of debate about future funding and management. The trouble with an XC track aimed at the world's best riders is that only the world's best riders can ride it as it was designed to be ridden. XC courses of this standard have a lot of climbing, some of which is technical, and technical descents. They are designed to test fitness and technical ability during repeated laps. That means they aren't always the greatest fun for leisure riders.

The park is also open to walkers, so be aware of other users. Livestock can also be present and aren't always known for their ability to read the signs about keeping off the trails.

Trails
■ **4 kilometres.** This is a shorter and easier option than the red, using some of the same tracks but with a separate loop at the bottom of the park. It does have some steep climbs, though. It's surfaced, so is an all-weather option.

■ **5 kilometres, with optional black features.** This is the legacy track itself. It is very much an XC course, but do not underestimate the six technical descent features. There are easier options around them. There's 1.7 kilometres of climbing in every lap. It is similarly surfaced to the blue trail, so again is an all-weather option.

Multi-use trails
■ **The Green Trail, 9 kilometres.** A family trail.
■ **The Purple Trail, 1.5 kilometres.** Another family trail.

Other features
There is also a skills area and pump track.

HADLEIGH COUNTRY PARK. © JOOLZE DYMOND

PHOENIX BIKE PARK

52.2724, 0.5159 / Bury Road, Kentford, Newmarket, Suffolk, CB8 7PZ / *www.phoenixcycleworks.co.uk*

Like most bike parks, the lines here are being developed and tweaked constantly. Gloves, eye protection and body armour are recommended, and helmets are compulsory. You will need a day pass to ride.

They have training available for all ages, plus evening and women-only sessions. They also hold occasional jam sessions advertised through their social media.

Trails
This is very much a jump park, with jumps of pretty much all sizes right from a balance bike pump track through to huge trickable jumps. This makes it a great place for progression – there's wall rides, whale tails, drops, tables, doubles, step-ups, step-downs, trick jumps, mulch and anything you require. The jump build is high quality as a fair number of pro riders play out here.

There is also a 2-kilometre XC trail round the outside of the site, but the emphasis really is on jumps.

THE DIRT DIRECTORY

THETFORD FOREST. © *JOOLZE DYMOND*

THETFORD FOREST. © *JOOLZE DYMOND*

THETFORD FOREST – HIGH LODGE

52.4345, 0.6636 / High Lodge, Thetford Forest, Brandon, Suffolk, IP27 0AF / *www.forestryengland.uk/high-lodge*

This is as flat as you might expect a trail centre in East Anglia to be, so whichever route you choose there will be lots of pedalling. There's not too much gnarliness here, but there is quite a bit of fun. It's a great place for those wanting a gentler introduction to off-roading.

If you'd like to get involved with trail maintenance, search out TIMBER MTB on Facebook.

Trails

■ **Beater Trail, 10 or 18 kilometres.** A gentle route with very little in the way of difficulty; it has the occasional shallow berm and twisty bit. Much of it is singletrack, although it is wider than the red trail.

■ **Lime Burner Trail, 16 kilometres.** This is pretty flat so is very pedally, but it does make the most of the terrain where it can, especially around the Beast, which is the most technical section. There is a signed return to the start of the Beast so it can be easily sessioned. A good, straightforward introduction for those new to red trails.

■ Mountain bike pits and features throughout the wood. These are mostly signed off the red route; one is signed off the Beast's return route. They are nothing overly spicy, but they can add a bit of fun to an easy ride.

Multi-use trails

■ Shepherd Trail, 5.5 or 8 kilometres.

TWISTED OAKS BIKE PARK AND TRAILS

52.0348, 1.2794 / Brightwell Road, Bucklesham, Ipswich, Suffolk, IP10 0AZ / *twistedoaks.co.uk*

Twisted Oaks is a constantly developing bike park with an emphasis on progression of riding

THE MIDLANDS & EAST ANGLIA

THETFORD FOREST. © *JOOLZE DYMOND*

TWISTED OAKS BIKE PARK AND TRAILS. © *JOOLZE DYMOND*

skills. Some trails are out in the open, others are in the woods. Their aim is to be family and beginner friendly, as well as offering bigger and more technical trails for the advanced rider. You will need membership or a day pass to ride.

Trails

■ **XC loop, 2.2 kilometres.** A broad track winding around the land, aimed at families and beginners.

■ **XC loop, 6.4 kilometres.** A surprisingly hilly XC loop with various features which can be included or avoided as you choose. Future extension plans will include even more features. XC races are also hosted here.

Other features

There are loads of jump lines of varying difficulty – you'll find everything from small and rollable to big and gappy. They are well built, with rider progression firmly in mind. Again, it's a place that's so well designed the pros come to play, and yet there are plenty of things for a beginner to practise on too. One really nice feature is a parallel line of tables and doubles – exactly the same length – so if you can clear the tables you can clear the doubles.

There is a dual slalom track, which is pretty big but with rollable features.

There's also a 4X track of a national standard so it can be used for racing.

TUNSTALL FOREST

52.1507, 1.4783 / Tunstall Road, Tunstall, Suffolk, IP12 2HQ / *www.forestryengland.uk/tunstall-forest* / Trail Maintenance: *www.trogmtb.com/viking-trail*

Tunstall Forest is well used by walkers and horse riders, so be aware and be thoughtful of them. There are bridleways and quiet roads connecting this forest to Rendlesham Forest, so you can include the Viking Trail as part of a longer ride around the area. The forest is also part of the Suffolk and Essex Coast and Heaths National Landscape.

THE DIRT DIRECTORY

TUNSTALL FOREST. © *JOOLZE DYMOND*

Trails

🟥 **Viking Trail, 16 kilometres.** An XC-style trail which certainly makes the most of the undulating terrain as it twists through the trees. Expect to pedal. Lots. There aren't many technical sections, but there are some avoidable bomb holes to play in. The trail holds water in winter and riding it is discouraged when the ground is really wet. It's graded red because of the width of the trail rather than any technical features, so is good for beginners.

Other features

There is also a small dirt jump park at Sudbourne (**52.1293, 1.5182**), but at the time of writing the management and access to this part of the wood is under discussion.

SKILLZ BIKE PARK

52.5219, 1.7351 / Stirrups Lane, Corton, Lowestoft, Suffolk, NR32 5LE / *www.skillzbikepark.co.uk*

A tiny bike park in Suffolk which styles itself as being very much a family friendly place. The emphasis is on skills development, so imagine a bigger version of a skills loop at a big bike park.

You will need to buy a ticket, or you can hire out the whole place for yourself and some friends. They do limit numbers on site because of the size so check ahead before you travel.

Trails

There are plenty of lines and obstacles to practise and session. It's set in an old pit, so there is a reasonable amount of elevation and drop for the area.

OPPOSITE TWISTED OAKS BIKE PARK AND TRAILS. © *JOOLZE DYMOND*

YORKSHIRE & THE HUMBER

Yorkshire and the Humber is an area with lots of good natural riding, from the Peak District to the Yorkshire Dales and North York Moors, so not as many constructed trails have been built here. There are quite a few places close to cities, though, which enables quality blasts for locals – Sheffielders are particularly spoilt in this respect.

1. Lady Canning's Plantation *p64*
2. Rother Valley Country Park *p65*
3. Parkwood Springs *p66*
4. Grenoside *p69*
5. Oakwell Hall *p69*
6. Leeds Urban Bike Park *p71*
7. Havok Bike Park *p72*
8. Stainburn *p72*
9. Sutton Bank *p74*
10. Dalby Forest *p76*

THE DIRT DIRECTORY

YORKSHIRE & THE HUMBER

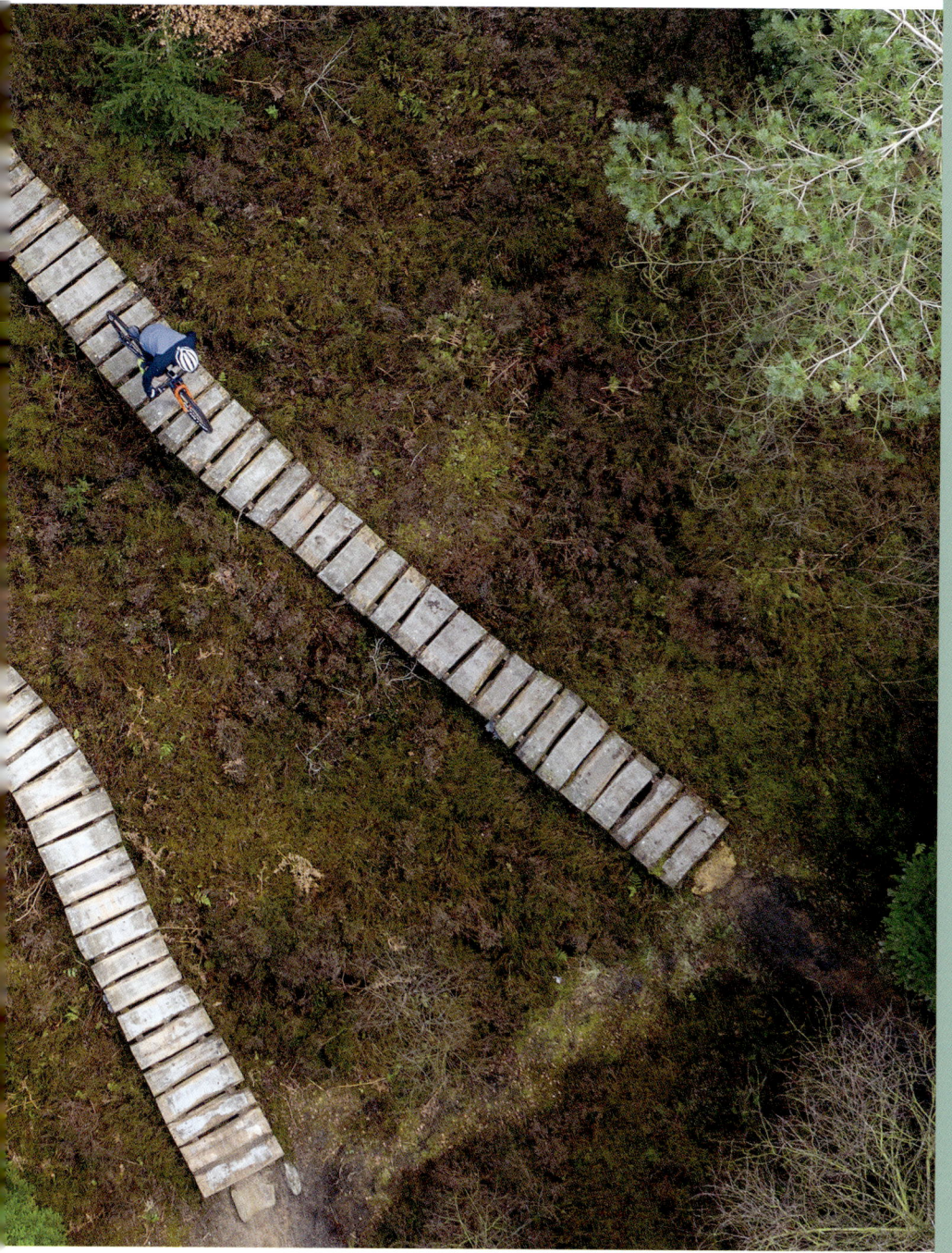

DALBY FOREST. © *JOOLZE DYMOND*

THE DIRT DIRECTORY

LADY CANNING'S PLANTATION. © *JOHN COEFIELD*

LADY CANNING'S PLANTATION. © *JOHN COEFIELD*

LADY CANNING'S PLANTATION

53.3472, -1.5653 / Sheephill Road, Sheffield, South Yorkshire, S11 7TU / *www.ridesheffield.org.uk/project/lady-cannings-plantation* / Trail maintenance: *www.ridesheffield.org.uk*

Lady Canning's Plantation is small but immense amounts of fun and is rightly very popular, especially in school holidays. The trails can be sessioned by themselves or included in a longer ride using some of the classic bridleway routes in the Dark Peak and the connecting routes from Sheffield.

Blue Steel was the first trail in the UK to be built using crowdfunded money, and so it's a pioneer in terms of how local groups and landowners can positively work together.

There are two trails, both of which start at the top of the wood. There is a kilometre of bridleway from the car park up to the start, which means loops are easy to do, or you can ride around the edge of the wood for better views. Lady Canning's is a great place for beginners and experienced riders alike, and despite the name sounding like a euphemism for a Victorian brothel, it is a great local resource.

Trails

■ **Cooking on Gas, 1.6 kilometres.** This trail is slightly more flowy in style than Blue Steel: there are lots of berms and rollers, and some small, rollable slab features. The features are slightly bigger than on Blue Steel, but are still all very manageable. At the time of writing (autumn 2024), it is showing signs of wear, but plans are afoot to upgrade the trail surface.

■ **Blue Steel, 1.4 kilometres.** A great beginner red trail – in fact, it is so named as it was originally graded blue. There are enough features to keep you interested, but everything can be rolled. The berms, rollers and very small drop-offs are useful for progressing your skills. Some of the rollers can be made into doubles if you are good enough.

LADY CANNING'S PLANTATION. © *JOHN COEFIELD*

ROTHER VALLEY COUNTRY PARK

53.3403, -1.3203 / Mansfield Road, Wales Bar, Sheffield, South Yorkshire, S26 5PQ (follow the signs, not the post code) / www.rvcp.co.uk / Trail maintenance: www.facebook.com/rothervalleyriders

There's loads of activities for families in the Rother Valley Country Park, so it does get busy at weekends and in school holidays. As part of the activities available there are several biking trails suitable for all ages and abilities, from pottering gently around the lake to more natural and techy stuff.

There are two sections of the woods containing trails, linked by an easy shared trail along the bottom of the valley. It's worth studying the trail map to work out exactly which bits you want to ride.

Trails other than Diggers Downhill have a natural feel, so expect slippery roots and some mud in wet conditions.

Trails

■ **4 kilometres.** This is a gentle ride along the valley with a relatively long climb, then an easy, XC-style descent. It's all pretty straightforward, although the climb can be tough on small legs.

■ **6.5 kilometres in total.** However, you can also pick and choose: head left out of the visitor centre to use the same approach and ascent as the blue trail into Drift Woods, where there is a singletrack XC-type course; heading right out of the centre brings you to Gravel Climb, which is exactly as its name suggests. It's a pretty steep gravel climb, but it is used to access the other trails which come off it.

Buzzard Banger is on the left of Gravel Climb as you head up and is an XC sort of trail. Further along the same access is Fort Elbow. Even further up the climb and on the right is the flow trail called **Diggers Downhill**, with rollers and berms and everything a flow trail should have.

■ **Fort Elbow, 1 kilometre.** Use Gravel Climb and Buzzard Banger to access this trail. It's naturally techy in feel.

Multi-use trails

■ **5 kilometres.** A pretty flat trail around the lake.

PARKWOOD SPRINGS. © *JOHN COEFIELD*   PARKWOOD SPRINGS. © *JOHN COEFIELD*

PARKWOOD SPRINGS

53.4016, -1.4705 / Shirecliffe Road, Sheffield, South Yorkshire, S5 8XB / www.ridesheffield.org.uk/project/parkwood-springs / Trail maintenance: *www.ridesheffield.org.uk*

Parkwood Springs is a 'wild' space not far from Sheffield city centre; a little oasis of the great outdoors in an otherwise built-up area. It's home to a handful of short trails – old and new – and it's easy to ride to from the city, which also means refreshments and facilities are not very far away; the trendy bars and restaurants of Kelham Island are just at the bottom of the hill. The car park is open daily but does close early evening; toilets are a relatively recent addition. If you are riding in from Sheffield city centre, you can also access the trails from Rutland Road.

The original 2-kilometre blue trail at the southern end of the Springs opened in 2012 and is holding up well; a fun, bermy, jumpy downhill linked by singletrack climbing. Good XC training. New for 2024, 500 metres to the north, linked by a multi-user trail, is a collection of smooth green, blue and red flow trails. The views of Sheffield from the trail between the two sites are fantastic.

Trails

🟩 **500 metres.** A steady XC loop at the lower end of the hill on broad, flowy singletrack without any nasty surprises.

🟦 **2 kilometres.** The original Parkwood trail. This has plenty of jumps, rollers and berms with a slightly more challenging red option on the descent. It's surfaced, so rides well in wet weather. It is perfect for laps.

🟦 **700 metres.** The 'new' blue downhill has two jumpy options at the top (easy to session), before plunging into the woods through big, sweeping berms. Lots of jumps and rollers; not a rock in sight. Climb back up on the multi-user trail for another run.

🟥 **380 metres.** The red downhill splits off from the new blue shortly after it has entered the woods and is a touch steeper and jumpier, yet still very flowy.

Other features

There is also a short but fun dual slalom track for settling arguments among friends, and a pump track for the anti-pedalling brigade.

OPPOSITE PARKWOOD SPRINGS. © *JOHN COEFIELD*

YORKSHIRE & THE HUMBER

GRENOSIDE. © PATRICK COEFIELD

GRENOSIDE

53.4507, -1.5116 / Woodhead Road, Wood Seats, Sheffield, South Yorkshire, S35 8RS / www.ridesheffield.org.uk/project/greno / Trail maintenance: www.ridesheffield.org.uk

Want to know why Steve Peat is such a good DH rider, especially in the mud? Come to Grenoside and Wharncliffe woods and find out for yourself. There are three waymarked trails in Greno itself, but across the road in Wharncliffe there are lots of other unwaymarked DH trails. There are also bridleways and the Trans Pennine Trail running through both woods, so be aware of other users. All of this does mean it's easy to ride into the trails as well.

Sheffield Wildlife Trust manages Grenoside Woods and has a good working relationship with the local riding community. Greno hosts Peaty's Steel City DH every year, and money from that race gets ploughed back into trail maintenance.

Trails

All three trails head down off the top bridleway, which loops round so you can ride/push up from the bottom. Most people come to session the short, but testing, tracks. Once you're on the push up you'll appreciate just how much descent there has been. These are quality and legendary trails.

■ **Pub Run, 650 metres.** The mellowest of the runs, but still quite techy. It's probably best to start on this to get the feel of the area if it's your first time. The trail has a few doubles and tables, but nothing that can't be rolled.

■/■ **Steel City, 800 metres.** The best known of the tracks, with some big features (all rollable or avoidable). Depending on how recently it's been resurfaced, it can be smooth and flowy or really quite rocky and gnarly. There are some split lines because of the large gap jumps, so make sure you know which line you are on. It leads down to the infamous bomb hole finish. A classic.

■ **DH3, 520 metres.** A trail with a DH/tech/enduro feel, with plenty of rocky sections but no unavoidable gaps. It's interesting to say the least on a hardtail. Again, it depends on how recently maintenance was done as to whether it's on the smoother or rockier side.

OAKWELL HALL

53.7391, -1.6712 / Warrens Lane, Birstall, West Yorkshire, WF17 9LG / www.facebook.com/OakwellHallMTBTrail / Trail maintenance: ridekirklees.wordpress.com or the Ride Kirklees Facebook group

Another wood where informal local trails have been made into a waymarked trail.

Trails

■ **1.4 kilometres.** A very short flow trail with some berms and rollers; there's a couple of rollable drop-offs towards the end and two small rock gardens at the end of each downhill section. There's a surprising amount of up for such a short trail. This is great as part of a longer local ride.

OPPOSITE GRENOSIDE. © JOHN COEFIELD

YORKSHIRE & THE HUMBER

LEEDS URBAN BIKE PARK. © JOOLZE DYMOND

LEEDS URBAN BIKE PARK

53.7521, -1.5585 / Ring Road, Leeds, West Yorkshire, LS10 3TN / www.leedsurbanbikepark.com

Although Leeds Urban Bike Park is called a bike park, unlike many other such establishments it is free to park and ride here (though the car park is locked out of hours). Middleton (Miggy) Woods had long been used for riding before the park was built, and there had been some relatively gnarly trails using the steepest part of the wood. Now the bike park has been built, though, it's a place pulled in two directions: the family users want decent easy trails suitable for trailers and small bikes; the local gnarly boys want big jumps to send. What's here tends to fall awkwardly between the two. It gets very busy on weekends and during school holidays.

Trails
■ Two short blue tracks, 700 metres each. One is slightly more of a jump line, with some flattering (as in, built to help you get over them) jumps and rollers.
■ Red trails. The first, shorter, trail leads up to the jump line via some berms and tables – you can then either try the big jump line or take the easier route back. If it is windy then note the jump line heads directly into the predominant wind direction and becomes even harder to ride well.

The longer XC red trail, which is approximately 3.5 kilometres, goes into the woods. It starts with some big jumps, which can be avoided or sessioned. This is a trail for those who can jump or who can flatten jumps in a controlled fashion. Some of the lips on jumps are rather steeper than you might expect on a red trail. There is one section where you will need to pick your line through: there is a series of doubles and drops, but it's hard to see the first time where the easiest line is. This section can easily be sessioned, though. This trail is very popular and well used, so expect erosion and braking bumps. It also includes black options at the quarry – two of the black options are rollable, the other is a definite drop and needs commitment. The return to the trailhead is a pretty draggy uphill.

Multi-use trails
■ 2.3 kilometres. This uses the tarmacked path around the park.

Other features
■ Pump track. This is small yet fun. It's definitely aimed at the smaller wheel sizes and BMXs.
■ BMX track. This has a variety of lines with different sizes of jumps. It tends to be used more as a jump spot rather than a BMX track.

OPPOSITE LEEDS URBAN BIKE PARK. © JOOLZE DYMOND

THE DIRT DIRECTORY

STAINBURN. © *JOOLZE DYMOND*

HAVOK BIKE PARK

53.7339, -2.1536 / Station Parade, Todmorden, West Yorkshire, OL14 8PU / www.havokmtb.co.uk

After a lot of hard work, Havok is back in its second incarnation after the first had to close in 2021 following storm damage and landowner issues. There are trails for all abilities and the rider-owned and operated park is constantly being worked on by the crew. Riding is currently weekends only – details on the website.

STAINBURN

53.9534, -1.6814 / Norwood, Otley, North Yorkshire, LS21 2RA / www.forestryengland.uk/stainburn / Trail maintenance: www.singletraction.co.uk

Stainburn is known for being rocky and technical. The runs are pretty short but pretty punchy – it's not a place to just go for a ride, but a place to session and to practise. Armour is probably a good idea – knee pads have prevented many a fall here from being a lot more serious. Guy Kesteven (opposite) rides here a lot testing bikes, and he's nicknamed it 'brutal "North YorkShore" (like old-school 'North Shore' but made out of drystone walls)'.

The trails hold water in winter. Expect greasy tree roots after rain and in winter, and rocks – lots of rocks.

Trails

■ **Ascent Line, 500 metres.** Fairly technical in places, with some rocks in interesting positions, the Red Ascent Line wiggles its way up to the top point of the lower wood. Strangely, it seems more technical at the bottom of the climb before mellowing into a series of switchbacks. There is then a choice of descents.

■ **Descent Line, 500 metres.** As you look down the hill this is the track on the left, parallel with the road, and is the easiest of the lines down, so it's a good place to start if this is your first time here or you want a warm-up. This is fairly swoopy, but it does have some rollable or avoidable rocky technical sections. There is then a line on the right with three drop-offs – choose your size – to cut back up to the red ascent. Or continue down to the car park.

■ **The Descent Line, 1 kilometre.** The line on the right from the top of the wood. It's rockier than the other red descent, with some interesting boulder sections which can be rolled or sent depending on your skills and confidence. You can cut across to the uphill access in places or continue to the bottom of the land.

■ **Warren Boulder Ascent, 1 kilometre.** From the bottom of the forest, you can either push up a fire road or you can come up a fairly tricky, techy ascent. See how they mention boulder in the title? That's not all you get, as there are roots and other delights on the trail as well.

■ **Warren Boulder Descent, 1.4 kilometres.** This starts at the car park and heads mostly downhill, although not always – there are some tricky ups as well. There are some very technical rocky sections and plenty of chances to get it wrong, and there are some very awkward corners. If in doubt as to where

OPPOSITE STAINBURN. © *JOOLZE DYMOND*

THE DIRT DIRECTORY

SUTTON BANK. © *JOHN LAVELLE*

the actual trail is, just ride over the rocks and you will usually be right. A pretty brutal descent.

Other features
There is a small pump track just off the car park, which is handy for a warm-up, although there is no doubt you will get warm on the ascents.

Across the road in the upper wood are lots of unmarked trails varying in length and technicality, but mostly with an enduro feel to them.

SUTTON BANK

54.2409, -1.2090 / Sutton Bank, Thirsk, North Yorkshire, YO7 2EH / www.suttonbankbikes.co.uk/trails

Sutton Bank is a pretty impressive escarpment at the western edge of the North York Moors National Park. The aim with the trails here is to bridge the gap between trail centres and natural riding, so while there are some purpose-built trails, the existing bridleway network is also used. The idea is that all the trails start the same way but that you pick the extension you fancy, which is then pretty clearly waymarked – as you'd expect from a trail centre. It's therefore an easy step to an XC ride but without navigational difficulties (although a map as backup will be handy).

Trails
■ **Cliff Trail, 5.5 kilometres.** This starts with the X Trail, which is a one-way, wide trail suitable for all. You can do loops of this, cut back to the visitor centre or continue to do the full 5 kilometres. There is a tiny bit of road work, then some easy trails across the fields to the escarpment.

■ **Fort Trail (short), 9.5 kilometres.** Like the green trail, this is all hard-packed surface so will ride well in any weather and it isn't technically difficult.

■ **Fort Trail (long), 13 kilometres.** This includes a long descent off the escarpment on the bridleways, which are of mixed terrain and can get wet and muddy. There is then a long haul back up on fire roads and bridleway, most of which is on a good surface. You then join the blue and green trails back to the visitor centre.

■/■ **Drovers Trail, 17 kilometres.** This is an extension of the longer blue, but it goes up on to the old Drove Road. Again, this is straightforward enough under wheel.

■ **Paradise Trail, 29 kilometres.** A classic XC ride with a lot more up and down. Expect a variety of tracks and surfaces, especially after wet weather.

Other features
■ **Skills area.** This is not particularly challenging.
Pump track. Accessed via the green Cliff Trail, it is very nicely built.

OPPOSITE SUTTON BANK. © *ANDY SCARSBROOK*

THE DIRT DIRECTORY

DALBY FOREST. © *JOHN COEFIELD*

DALBY FOREST

Visitor Centre: **54.2755, -0.6868** / Low Dalby, Thornton-Le-Dale, Pickering, North Yorkshire, YO18 7LT / Dixon's Hollow car park: **54.2961, -0.6424** / Allerston, Pickering, Yorkshire, YO18 7LR
www.forestryengland.uk/dalby-forest / Trail maintenance: www.singletraction.co.uk

Dalby is really known for its XC stuff; most of it was built when long and not too technical was the main style of riding. If that's your thing, there is plenty for you here; if you are looking for gnarly enduro stuff, then you won't find it waymarked. There are also lots of bridleways crossing the local area, so it's possible to include Dalby as part of a longer ride.

The forest is also used for events – XC, gravel and endurance events have all been run here.

Trails
■ **Jubilee Trail, 11 kilometres from the visitor centre.** This involves a long climb to the start on a mix of singletrack and fire road. Then there's a mix of mainly flowy singletrack and more fire road undulating back to the car park.

■ **Full red trail, 34.3 kilometres.** This is clearly a long haul for many people; there is a lot of climbing and it's not a short day out. It's known as a 'classic XC route', which some feel is a euphemism for 'long and boring', depending on your riding preference. If you want a long day out in the saddle while not being overly taxed by technical sections, you may well enjoy this. There's a couple of spicier sections, such as Medusa's Drop, to keep you on your toes. However, you can also split the trail up into three much more manageable sections:

Jerry Noddle Trail, 11.1 kilometres from Dixon's Hollow car park.

Newclose Rigg, 9.6 kilometres from the visitor centre.

Riggs and Dales, 13.8 kilometres from the visitor centre.

■ **World Cup MTB trail, 6.4 kilometres from Dixon's Hollow.** This is short, but it includes steep, challenging climbs, drops of various sizes and technical, rooty downs. In short, it's what you can expect from a world cup course. Channel your inner Nick Craig to make the most of it.

Multi-use trails
■ **Ellerburn Trail, 2.8 kilometres**, or 4.5 kilometres from the visitor centre.
■ **Adderstone Trail, 12.8 kilometres**, or 19.3 kilometres from Dixon's Hollow car park.

Other features
■ **Skills area.** This is accessed from the Ellerburn Trail.

There are also some off-piste trails in the forest.

OPPOSITE DALBY FOREST. © *JOHN COEFIELD*

NORTHERN ENGLAND

Northern England has a fair old mix of constructed trails: some of the big, long-ride type such as Kielder and Hamsterley, others designed to appeal to the gnarr seeker, such as Danny Hart's Descend Bike Park and Farmer Johns MTB Park, plus shorter, more local runs. In other words, there's probably something to suit your riding somewhere in the north.

1. Farmer Johns MTB Park *p82*
2. Clayton Vale *p82*
3. Philips Park *p83*
4. Pimbo Bike Park *p83*
5. Healey Nab *p83*
6. Billinge Wood *p83*
7. Rossendale *p85*
8. Gisburn Forest *p87*
9. Grizedale *p87*
10. Whinlatter *p88*
11. Danny Hart's Descend Bike Park *p91*
12. Hamsterley *p91*
13. Chopwell *p92*
14. Kielder *p92*

NORTHERN ENGLAND

ROSSENDALE. © *JOOLZE DYMOND*

THE DIRT DIRECTORY

FANJO. © SOPHIE FLETCHER

FARMER JOHNS. © SOPHIE FLETCHER

FARMER JOHNS MTB PARK

53.4108, -2.0452 / 57 Cote Green Road, Marple Bridge, Stockport, Greater Manchester, SK6 5EN / *fjmtb.com*

You will need to be a member or buy a day pass to ride here. Full-face helmets are compulsory, and armour is recommended. There's no uplift, so you'll have to push.

There's also plenty of DH racing and events held here – details on the website.

Trails

There is a range of DH/enduro-based tracks here for the more experienced and confident rider. They are not for the beginner or the terrified, but for the confident it can be a good place for progression. There are several variant tracks with linking trails depending on what John has been digging, so expect frequent tweaks to the lines. There's plenty of variety in the tracks, with features including flowy sections, big berms, steep and techy woods, rock gardens, jumps and North Shore, so there should be something to suit you. Start on the nice, flowy and jumpy warm-up track and you'll soon get your eye in.

Other features

There's also a dirt jump section, so there is plenty of chances to get your wheels off the ground on all sizes of jumps. Some are rollable, others large and committing.

CLAYTON VALE

53.4857, -2.1911 / Stuart Street, Manchester, Greater Manchester, M11 4DQ / *www.nationalcyclingcentre.com/mtb*

The National Cycling Centre in Manchester has a velodrome of international standard and a BMX track of national standard, plus some MTB trails. Due to the size of the land available, all of the MTB tracks are pretty short, and, despite the location, maintenance isn't great. The trails feel more like an afterthought to the other tracks. You'll probably get more from the public track and BMX sessions.

Trails

■ **Clayton Vale Easy Rider, 4 kilometres.** This is the easiest trail – wide and rollable – and is suitable for most bikes; it connects to all the other trails.

■ **Newton Heath Sidewinder, 4 kilometres.** This has a few more features, with some rollers and berms on the trail.

■ **Urban Red Rock-it.** This comes off the blue trail and adds a little more technicality, with some small drop-offs, rock gardens and steeper gradients.

■ **Scorpions Tail.** A short section of more technical track off the red trail, but still nothing too extreme.

All of the XC trails share some sections with each other – a trail map is available.

Other features

■ Skills zone with a pump track.

NORTHERN ENGLAND

PHILIPS PARK

53.5342, -2.3058 / Prestwich, Manchester, Greater Manchester, M45 7QJ / *www.bury.gov.uk/local-leisure-events/nature-reserves/philips-park*

This park just off the M60 in north-west Manchester suffers from intermittent funding and maintenance and doesn't have the best waymarking. It does connect to National Cycle Network route 6, though.

Trails

■ **Waterdale Trail, 3 kilometres.** This is a flatter trail in the valley bottom, if you can find it. It is a good mix of singletrack and fire roads.

■ **Philips Park Figure 8 Trail, 3.5 kilometres.** This comprises two downs with some jumps and berms; a road climb links the two downs with the car park.

PIMBO BIKE PARK

53.5368, -2.7762 / Whiteledge Road, Skelmersdale, Lancashire, WN8 9QF / *pimbobikepark.co.uk*

Pimbo is a constantly developing small bike park with an emphasis on jumps and flow. It's a great place to develop your jumping skills. If you are trying the jumps, protection is probably wise, and you must sign in on arrival.

Trails

Pimbo has a variety of sizes of jump lines, allowing good progression with jumping and cornering skills. They are graded from blue to black, from rollable tables to sendable gaps. There's lots of variety and lots to session and progress on, with something for most abilities of jumpers.

There are also some short XC loops, beginning with a green with red and black options/sections.

Other features

There is a dual slalom track.

HEALEY NAB

53.6576, -2.5955 / Moor Road, Anglezarke, Chorley, Lancashire, PR6 9BU / *www.visitlancashire.com/things-to-do/healey-nab-mountain-bike-trails-p746070* / Trail maintenance: I Dig Healey Nab Facebook page

There is a permissive access track to the trails off the bridleway called Heapey Fold Lane (**53.656, -2.5900**). You'll have to ride in. There are no facilities here, although Chorley is just the other side of the M61.

Trails

■/■ There are several fairly natural-feeling trails from the top of the hill. These can vary depending on what digging has been going on, but expect rock, roots, mud if it's been wet, drop-offs and a few jumps. They are fairly short descents which can be sessioned using the climb. The dig team are pretty active, so expect tweaks and changes on a regular basis. If it is wet, the local sandstone will act as a grinding paste on your brake pads and transmission.

BILLINGE WOOD

53.7494, -2.5211 (53.7389, -2.5135 – Witton Park car park; **53.7363, -2.5231** – Pleasington Playing Fields car park. A concessionary bridleway leads up to the woods from either spot. You can also access the wood from Billinge End Road or Under Billinge Lane.) / Billinge End Road, Blackburn, Lancashire, BB2 6QA / *www.pmba.org.uk/billinge-woods*

There are only a couple of short trails here, which are possibly best included as part of a longer local ride. It's popular with other users too, so be aware.

Trails

■ **Tricky 60, 250 metres; Two Trees, 300 metres.**

These are two short descent tracks, which are fairly natural feeling, linked by a multi-use track which allows for sessioning. There is a perennial problem with missing signage.

NORTHERN ENGLAND

ROSSENDALE. © JOHN COEFIELD

ROSSENDALE

There are two quarries at Rossendale containing trails, linked by a bridleway up the moor, but if you visit Cragg Quarry you'll probably be going to Lee Quarry as well, hence they are listed together here. There is about 100 metres of ascent from the car park to Lee Quarry, and then about another 100 metres of ascent up to Cragg Quarry. It can be windy and exposed by the time you get to the top – be prepared in terms of clothing and refreshments.

LEE QUARRY

53.6854, -2.2074 / Futures Park, Bacup, Lancashire, OL13 0BB / *www.pmba.org.uk/lee-cragg-quarries* / Trail maintenance: *www.pmba.org.uk*

Lee Quarry is a popular venue for racing, from XC to more enduro-based stuff.

Parking can be found around **53.6923, -2.2086** – follow the straight, steep climb up to the quarry itself.

Trails
■ There is a red trail which is intermittently marked through the quarry. However, the quarry itself is full of lines and the best riding is found by exploring and riding what you fancy. It is loose, rocky, steep and excellent for practising the tech/enduro/DH end of things. It's probably advisable to wear protection. This is not a place for the unconfident.

■ There are a couple of black sections labelled as alternatives to the red.

CRAGG QUARRY

53.6717, -2.2348 / Futures Park, Bacup, Lancashire, OL13 0BB / *www.pmba.org.uk/lee-cragg-quarries* / Trail maintenance: *www.pmba.org.uk*

There is a track linking the south-west corner of Lee Quarry with Cragg Quarry on the moor above – it's about 3 kilometres long. This is partly purpose built and partly the old tracks used by the Pennine Bridleway. On the way back down to Lee Quarry you can, if you wish, take advantage of the boulders placed cunningly along the sides of the track and practise your drop-offs.

Around the corner from Futures Park is Stubbylee Park, with a short pump track and toilets.

Trails
■ **5.5 kilometres.** This can be quite hard to follow in places. It has a slightly more XC feel than Lee Quarry, but is still quite rocky and loose in places. These are not groomed trails. It can be included as part of a longer ride using the Pennine Bridleway and Rooley Moor. Handily, Vertebrate Publishing also do a guide to the Pennine Bridleway (*Pennine Bridleway* by Hannah Collingridge – me!).

OPPOSITE ROSSENDALE. © JOHN COEFIELD

NORTHERN ENGLAND

GRIZEDALE. © ANDY SCARSBROOK

GISBURN FOREST

53.9993, -2.3891 / Stephen Park, Clitheroe, Lancashire, BB7 4TS / *www.forestryengland.uk/gisburn-forest-and-stocks* / Trail maintenance: *www.pmba.org.uk*

Gisburn Forest has a mix of surfaced and more natural trails. It's a popular place, so it does get hammered and therefore can suffer from a lack of maintenance. It holds water after wet periods and the natural trails can become a bit of a mud bath.

Trails
- **Bottoms Beck Trail, 9.5 kilometres.** This is on the flowy and not-too-technical side.
- **The 8, 18 kilometres** with some black options. This includes some of the blue route on the first loop of the figure of eight. There's a mix of surfaces, including rocks, roots, boardwalk, more rocks, more roots, smooth, flowy trail and often mud and water. Not for nothing is it known as one of the wettest trail centres known to biking kind. There are some sections of fire road in between the singletrack sections.
- **Big Foot Slab and Hully Gully.** These both come off the red route as options. The former is a slabby, rocky chute; the latter is a line of big berms down a gully.
- **Hope Line, 500 metres.** This trail has berms, tables and a few drop-offs. This is the track that Hope Technology paid for, hence the name. It's quite flowy if it's not too eroded at the time you visit.
- **Leap of Faith, 500 metres.** A steeper, rougher line with drops and unavoidable gaps. Not for the unconfident.

Other features
There's also a skills loop.

GRIZEDALE

54.3407, -3.0230 / Grizedale Forest, Ambleside, Cumbria, LA22 0QJ / *www.forestryengland.uk/grizedale*

Grizedale has been kind of ignored by Forestry England since it was built and has not really developed beyond the one trail. They've concentrated much more on appealing to families by laying out trails on the fire roads instead.

Trails
- **The North Face MTB Trail, 16 kilometres.** This has been around a long time and is of the 'sections of singletrack linked by long sections of fire road' style. There's some boardwalk and some rocky sections, but it doesn't get muddy so can be ridden all year round. But there is an awful lot of fire road and not much reward for it.
- **The Black MTB Trail, 1 kilometre.** A short, more technical run, with some loose, rocky sections.

Multi-use trails
There are several marked trails of varying length on fire roads throughout the forest.

Numerous bridleways run through the forest, and these offer a variety of excellent natural riding.

OPPOSITE GISBURN FOREST. © ANDY SCARSBROOK

THE DIRT DIRECTORY

WHINLATTER. © JOHN COEFIELD

WHINLATTER. © SOPHIE FLETCHER

WHINLATTER

54.6094, -3.2272 / Whinlatter Pass, Keswick, Cumbria, CA12 5TW / www.forestryengland.uk/whinlatter

At Whinlatter you should expect a fair amount of climbing and plenty of rocks. This does mean the trails are pretty robust and don't suffer too much from the wet weather. Billed by Forestry England as 'England's only true mountain forest', recent felling has really opened up the views which are utterly glorious on a good day.

Trails

■ **Quercus Trail, 3.5 or 7.5 kilometres.** This starts past the bike shop. There's plenty of flowy singletrack and it is a good place for getting newbies on to singletrack trails. Like all the best blues, it can be rolled or pinned depending on your skills. And the shortcut is handy if it's not for you.

■ **Altura Trail, 19 kilometres.** This is split into the South Loop and the North Loop. **South Loop, 9 kilometres.** This starts on the other (south) side of the road from the visitor centre. The top section is graded black. The trail is a mix of singletrack and fire road climbing. The top black section has plenty of rocky technical sections – beware of the rock when it's wet. The lower red section is fast and flowy with several jumps.

North Loop, 10 kilometres. This starts past the bike shop. The climb up to the top is a mix of singletrack and fire road, with perhaps too much fire road in the mix. Then the trail undulates on twisty singletrack with technical ups and downs before coming out of the woods for the final swoopy descent.

Multi-use trails

■ **Gorse Cycle Trail, 10 kilometres** on forest roads.

OPPOSITE WHINLATTER. © ALLAN EVANS

NORTHERN ENGLAND

DANNY HART'S DESCEND BIKE PARK

54.6551, -1.8993 / Windy Bank Road, Bishop Auckland, County Durham, DL13 3QN / www.descendbikepark.com

This is Danny Hart's place, which should give you an idea of the tendencies of the trails. If you have ever wondered why Danny has thrived on the steeper, muddier DH tracks, this place will give you a hint. It's a chance to play in a world champion's backyard.

Although Descend Bike Park is within Hamsterley Forest, it is in a separate part of it. You can turn up and pay on the day. Do not be an idiot and ride here without signing on.

You will need a full-face helmet to ride, and armour is highly recommended. Check out the park rules on the website. Uplift can be prebooked or you can walk/ride back up.

Trails

There are many trails and many variations here. In general, the top tracks are easier, faster and flowier, and then the bottom half gets more technical and rocky. None of it is particularly easy, and there is very much a focus on enduro/DH, with committing gaps, jumps and drops. It is not for the beginner or the unconfident. However, if steep and techy is your thing, you could have a great day here.

The trails are all graded from one dot orange through to what are pretty much pro lines. Start on the easier tracks to get warmed up and get an idea of what the place is about. Like most bike parks, there is always development and always tweaking of old trails, so what you rode last time may well be different this trip. DH and enduro races are held here on a reasonably regular basis.

Other features

There's also a 4X track.

HAMSTERLEY

54.6762, -1.8589 / Bedburn, Hamsterley, County Durham, DL13 3NL / www.forestryengland.uk/hamsterley-forest / Trail maintenance: www.hamsterley-trailblazers.co.uk

Hamsterley is a funny mix of old- and new-school trail building. Much is fire road, and it's worth studying the trail map in order to get to the best bits without kilometres of fire road climbing – it also means you can link the black and red trails.

Trails

■ **22 kilometres.** The majority of the red trail is fire road, with very little single-track until you get to Poulty's Last Blast. However, careful reading of the forest map means you can head directly to the interesting sections of Poulty's, K-Line, Transmission, Accelerator and Nitrous, which are more modern-style trails with a mix of jumps, berms, rollers and flow. There are some pretty sizeable jumps on K-Line for a normal trail centre. These sections are a lot of fun and can quite easily be sessioned using the fire roads to loop back round. Not slogging round all of the fire roads beforehand also means you won't be shattered by the time you get to the fun stuff.

■ **11 kilometres.** This has a more natural feel than the red trail, with plenty of roots in places. There's some quite interesting techy sections in places, especially on a hardtail. Careful map reading means you can join this on to sections of the red trail, too.

Multi-use trails

■ **14.5 kilometres.** This is all fire road.

DANNY HART'S DESCEND BIKE PARK.
© SOPHIE FLETCHER

OPPOSITE HAMSTERLEY. © ANDY SCARSBROOK

THE DIRT DIRECTORY

KIELDER. © JOOLZE DYMOND

CHOPWELL

54.9203, -1.7870 / Rowlands Gill, Gateshead, Tyne and Wear, NE39 1LT / *www.forestryengland.uk/chopwell-wood*

There are only two official trails here, but there is also plenty of off-piste riding in the wood if you can find it. The pump track nearby is great fun.

Trails

■ **Powerline, 1.5 kilometres** of mostly down. This is a short, mostly natural-feeling trail, and therefore it can be slippery in wet weather; it can get sloppy in the wet and retain water in places. There are some jumps and rollers. The trail runs under the big electricity transmission line, hence the name.

■ **Article 50, 500 metres.** This comes off Powerline near the top and rejoins the main trail before the bottom loop. Again, this trail has a natural feel and you should expect sketchiness when it's damp.

Both trails follow a fire road climb for 1.5 kilometres back up to the top, so sessioning is easy.

Other features
There's also a pump track (**54.9174, -1.8135**).

KIELDER

55.2358, -2.5798 / Kielder, Hexham, Northumberland, NE48 1ER / *www.forestryengland.uk/kielder-castle*

There are many, many miles of trails at Kielder, and as well as being a trail centre it's been used for many long-distance events. You can make your ride as long as you want here and connect to several other valleys – the Cross Border trail, for instance, goes to Newcastleton (p134). Kielder is regularly used for events such as XC marathons and endurance races, and for many years was the home of the iconic Kielder 100.

Trails

■ **Osprey Trail, 19 kilometres.** This is a mix of fire road and singletrack, which is not overly technical. It can get slippery in wet weather. It joins the Lakeside Way Trail towards the end of the loop.

■ **Lonesome Pine, 18 kilometres.** This climbs up one valley and descends another using a mix of flowy singletrack, fire roads and a huge section of wide boardwalk. The Lakeside Way Trail is used to join the ride up into a round.

■ **Bloody Bush Trail, 32 kilometres.** This is an extension to Lonesome Pine, looping up to the old border crossing of Bloody Bush. It can get very exposed on the tops, so be prepared.

■ **Deadwater Trail, 10.5 kilometres.** This trail comprises mostly fire road climb with some singletrack sections – it's not straight up, but it undulates. There's a pretty flowy singletrack descent with the occasional trail feature to be aware of, but there are also a couple of climbs in the descent – it's clearly a theme.

■ **Deadwater Up and Over Trail, 17.5 kilometres.** This shares the red trail's climb before going further up and therefore further down. Again, there's a lot of fire road climbing and the first descent is a wide, rough track. The next singletrack has drops, jumps and rock gardens.

Multi-use trails

■ **Borderline Trail, 11 kilometres.**
■ **Lakeside Way Trail, 42 kilometres.** This is not difficult, it's just long.

Other features
■ There is a skills park.

OPPOSITE KIELDER. © JOOLZE DYMOND

WALES

Wales has some great natural riding, but not as much as Scotland due to the access laws in England and Wales. However, Wales makes up for it with some of the best bike parks in the land, catering for every style of riding you could ever fancy.

1. Margam Country Park *p98*
2. Afan Forest Park *p100*
3. Dare Valley Gravity Bike Park *p102*
4. BikePark Wales *p103*
5. Mountain View Bike Park *p106*
6. Cwmcarn *p107*
7. Dirt Farm *p107*
8. Hafod Trails *p108*
9. Brechfa *p108*
10. Cwm Rhaeadr *p108*
11. Bwlch Nant yr Arian *p110*
12. Caersws Bike Park *p110*
13. Dyfi Bike Park *p111*
14. Dyfi Forest *p112*
15. Coed y Brenin *p115*
16. Revolution Bike Park *p116*
17. One Giant Leap DH *p116*
18. Coed Llandegla *p118*
19. Antur 'Stiniog *p121*
20. Penmachno *p122*
21. Gwydir *p122*
22. Marsh Tracks *p122*

THE DIRT DIRECTORY

BIKEPARK WALES. © ANDY LLOYD/BIKEPARK WALES

THE DIRT DIRECTORY

AFAN FOREST PARK. © *JOHN COEFIELD*

MARGAM COUNTRY PARK

51.5609, -3.7295 / Margam, Neath Port Talbot, SA13 2TJ / *www.margamcountrypark.co.uk*

This is a country park based around a 19th-century castle and gardens, so it has corresponding family attractions and events in school holidays.

The bike trails can be ridden when the park is open. These are all trails designed to appeal to the people visiting the country park, and thus are graded accordingly. There's nothing too gnarly or technical here, but the country park does get used for XC racing.

Trails
■ **5 kilometres**, including the green multi-use trail. There is some climbing on fire roads and then a pleasant flowy singletrack descent. Or you can cut out the green and just play on the blue descent.

■ **4 kilometres** as a loop on its own. Beware of the deer gates. A fire road climb leads to a singletrack descent, which is followed by more pleasant singletrack both up and down. There's nothing really technical here; a bit of steepness and the odd rollable drop-off. At the top of the last climb continuing on to the Pulpit will take you to the start of the black descents.

■ **Three descents** that can be added to the red. A little bit more technical but nothing too severe.

Multi-use trails
■ **A 4-kilometre family trail**, with wide, flat paths.

OPPOSITE MARGAM COUNTRY PARK. © *MAN DOWN MEDIA*

THE DIRT DIRECTORY

AFAN FOREST PARK/AFAN ARGOED

www.afanforestpark.com

There is loads of riding at Afan, from the flat and gentle to the definitely not flat or gentle. Plus, there are waymarked walks and a bunch of historical sites, so there's plenty of other things to do. Some of the riding is a little old school (singletrack plus loads of fire road) but there is plenty of good stuff too. It's a regular host for national 4X rounds and plenty of enduros too.

There are two main starting points for the several trails here. The two centres are also connected by the green-graded Rheilffordd Trail. Plus, there is a small bike park which has its own car park or is accessible from Y Wâl.

AFAN FOREST PARK VISITOR CENTRE

51.6422, -3.7054 / Cyonville, Port Talbot, Neath Port Talbot, SA13 3HG

GLYNCORRWG MOUNTAIN BIKE CENTRE

51.6739, -3.6310 / Ynyscorrwg Park, Glyncorrwg, Port Talbot, Neath Port Talbot, SA13 3EA

Trails
From Afan:

 Rookie, 6.1 kilometres. The 6.1-kilometre green section is wide and sweeping, with a 2.6-kilometre blue extension as a taster for something a bit harder. This is great for the unconfident and beginners.

■ **Blue Scar, 7 kilometres.** This includes a fair amount of climbing, but therefore a fair bit of descending too. There's a chunk of fire road in the middle of the route but also a good amount of flowy singletrack, with some easy trail features. This is a good beginner trail.

■ **Penhydd, 14.4 kilometres.** This starts along Blue Scar, but climbs further up the valley; there is a chunk of fire road work on this route. It's fairly flowy and not too technical, but is rocky in places. It rejoins the blue to finish.

■ **Y Wâl (the Wall), 23 kilometres.** This is the longer red with some black sections coming off it. There's plenty of climbing, plenty of singletrack, and plenty of fast and flowy descents. Again, it's rocky in places. The black options are steep and loose.

From Glyncorrwg:

■ **White's Level, 15.2 kilometres.** This is a more technical trail than the reds from Afan. There is lots of tight, twisty singletrack and more jumps and drops. It's a fairly technical climb to start with.

■ **Blade, 23 kilometres.** This splits off from White's Level after sharing parts of the climb. It then adds in some more climbing for good measure. The final descents are loose, rocky and fairly technical.

■ **Skyline Loop, 23 kilometres (plus Blade).** This is an extra as an add-on to the Blade. Much of the extended route is on fire roads, but it's the views rather than the singletrack that make this ride. It's a big day out so make sure you are prepared.

■ **W², 44 kilometres.** This route is a way to join the Y Wâl and White's Level trails together for a 44-kilometre ride. Start either at Glyncorrwg or Afan; the other will be halfway round the route for refreshments. If you need to bail, the Rheilffordd Trail is an easy way back.

AFAN BIKE PARK

51.6457, -3.7251 / Bryn Bettws Lodge, Port Talbot, Neath Port Talbot, SA12 9SP

There are several skills lines, plus jump lines ranging in size and difficulty. This starts with the fast and flowy trails and works its way up to fast, flowy trails with jumps. A nice area to session.

OPPOSITE AFAN FOREST PARK. © ANDY SCARSBROOK

DARE VALLEY GRAVITY BIKE PARK. © MAN DOWN MEDIA

DARE VALLEY GRAVITY BIKE PARK

51.7125, -3.4699 / Aberdare, Rhondda Cynon Taf, CF44 7PT / *darevalleygravity.co.uk*

Sensing that not everyone who wants uplift also wants gnarly trails, Dare Valley offers a range of blue flow trails and several pump tracks aimed at families, beginners and intermediate riders. It's all focused on the flow, so while there are jumps, they are all rollable. It's a brilliant idea, and because all the trails are blue you aren't fighting for uplift with the gnarr shredders.

There's coaching available for all ages, and plenty of events for families during school holidays and at weekends.

Trails

There's uplift (book via the website) or a steep ride to the top, and then several ways to get to the bottom. All of the descents here are graded blue, so offer variations in rollers and berms, flow and fun. It's a great way to push yourself a little without getting out of your depth.

Other features

There are several pump tracks.

BIKEPARK WALES. © ANDY LLOYD/BIKEPARK WALES

BIKEPARK WALES

51.7216, -3.3768 / Abercanaid, Merthyr Tydfil, CF48 1YZ /
www.bikeparkwales.com

BikePark Wales (BPW) is rightly popular. It can cater for pretty much any sort of riding you care to do, and if you are in a mixed-ability group you can all have a great day out. There's constant development and tweaking so it's likely there'll be something new or refreshed on your next visit. As long as you are happy going downhill, you will end up with a smile on your face – there is so much to choose from. And because there's such a variety of trails, there are plenty of chances to progress your riding. The trails are quite often split by the fire road running across the hill, which means you aren't necessarily committed to one grade all the way down – you can switch from one to another.

You will need to sign a waiver and book *before* your visit. You can either ride up (it's a long way – a *very long* way) or book uplift on the website. In terms of booking, there are a few options: experienced riders can just go straight for a day ticket, but there are a couple of packages aimed at novices, including gear hire

OPPOSITE PHOTO CAPTION TO BE CONFIRMED. © NAME SURNAME

THE DIRT DIRECTORY

BIKEPARK WALES. © WILL EVANS/BIKEPARK WALES

BIKEPARK WALES. © SARAH MUNTON/BIKEPARK WALES

options if you are new to mountain biking and want more guidance. There are also plenty of coaching courses available, again right across the board from beginners to the more experienced, and of course the park has all the trails you need to practise your new skills. Armour is recommended for the harder trails.

Trails
There are over 40 trails at BPW of all grades and for all abilities, from green to pro line. Everything is really carefully graded and described, so you know what you are getting into. There's even a 5-kilometre green trail (blue anywhere else) from the top of the hill, serving as an excellent introduction both to the park and for families and the unconfident. Realising that 5 kilometres is a long way for anyone not used to it, there are even rest points built in for a breather on the way down. It's that kind of detail that makes BPW so special.

Trails are split according to grade, but also by their general overall characteristic of 'flow' or 'tech', or alternatively 'blend', which contain an equal mixture of flow and techy features. This allows you to choose a trail according to your preferred style of riding. Don't be put off by the number of blue trails – these are well worth riding and are usually less cut up than the red trails. They are well-built blues and can be rolled or pinned according to your ability. While the lower-grade flow trails have features that can all be rolled, in the higher grades there will be unavoidable gaps and features that need speed and confidence to get right.

'Tech' trails are rockier, rootier and more technical than the flow trails – many of the reds come under tech. Expect a challenge if you want to ride them well, and if you are on a hardtail, **Rim Dinger** will ding more than your rim. That's all.

The harder the grade, the steeper, rootier and rockier it all gets. **50 Shades of Black** is rightly legendary, with a little bit of everything.

Vanta is the pro jump line, and home to the Red Bull Vanta Jam, which most of the UK's dirt jumpers attend. There are huge jumps, accompanied by huge air time.

Can't decide what you fancy? There are trails which are a bit of both flow and tech. Want to get your wheels off the ground? Look out for plus trails, which contain a higher proportion of jumps, drops or gaps.

There are races and events here as well. It's a great place for every kind of rider and every kind of riding.

OPPOSITE BIKEPARK WALES. © ANDY LLOYD/BIKEPARK WALES

THE DIRT DIRECTORY

CWMCARN. © *DEREK FOLMER*

MOUNTAIN VIEW BIKE PARK

51.5544, -3.2376 / Heol-Pen-y-Bryn, Caerphilly Mountain, Rhondda Cynon Taf, CF83 1NG / www.mountainviewbikepark.co.uk

The emphasis at Mountain View Bike Park is on progression, whatever age you are and whatever sort of riding you like to do. You will need to register and sign a waiver and then buy a day pass to ride. The park is continually developing, so new lines will appear.

The bike park offers plenty of coaching sessions for all ages, and stuff for kids during the school holidays.

This might be a small park, but it's great for advancing your riding.

Trails
There are XC-style lines through the woods with lots of options all coming off the basic blue trail: North Shore, small drops, berms, rollers. All can be avoided, if necessary, or used for progression.

Other features
There are a couple of pump tracks and then several jump lines. Again, the emphasis here is on progression, so they start small and end up big. You will find a jump of a size to suit you.

CWMCARN

51.6359, -3.1141 / Cwmcarn Forest Drive, Newport, NP11 7FA / www.mbwales.com/agents/cwmcarn

There's nothing really for absolute beginners here, but plenty for the reasonably confident rider as long as you have the fitness to get up the hills. The trails include great views on a good weather day, and driving rain and misery on a bad. Both the red trails do climb a long way up from the trailhead and can feel quite exposed, so make sure you are prepared in terms of supplies. There are also off-piste enduro tracks locally, and races of a gravity nature held here. The Cwmdown uplift closed down in 2023.

Trails

■ **Pwca, 3.3 kilometres.** This shares the outbound trail with the reds before splitting off and continuing to climb on undulating singletrack. It does have a steep drop on the side of the trail, so beware if that's not your thing. The trail is also relatively steep for absolute beginners. If you are confident, it's fast and flowy with a couple of rollers and tables. Sadly, it's also far too short.

■ The two red trails are on either side of the valley, but there is a link to join them.

Cafall, 15 kilometres. There is a long climb to start, along with some fire road, some singletrack and some undulating sections. Then it is mostly descent on twisting singletrack, which is fast and flowy with the odd technical section and looser trail. There's another climb in the middle, but then more of the good stuff – and more views. This is the slightly longer, higher and techier of the two reds.

Twrch, 13.3 kilometres. Again, this trail involves lots of climbing, sometimes on singletrack, sometimes on fire road and at times undulating. But there is eventually plenty of descent of the fast and flowy, not-too-technical variety. A few rollers and tables can be jumped or rolled. If you are reasonably fit, then it's a great beginner red.

■ **Pedalhounds DH track, 1.4 kilometres.** Access to this trail is via the Cafall trail. It's not the gnarliest DH trail ever, so reasonable-standard enduro riders should be okay. It is best to wear armour though. Expect roots, tight bits, fast bits, loose bits, drops and some jumps at the bottom.

■ **Y Mynydd DH track, 5 kilometres.** This is accessible via the forest roads. There are a couple of options at the top, one flowier, one rockier. It has some steep, loose sections and then big jumps towards the end. Everything can be rolled with care and the larger jumps can be bypassed, but that's not really the point. This is the gnarlier of the two DH trails. Armour and full-face helmets are recommended.

DIRT FARM

51.8855, -2.9825 / Great Llwygy Farm, Abergavenny, Monmouthshire, NP7 7PE / dirtfarm.wales

Formerly known as Black Mountains Cycle Centre, Dirt Farm has a range of tracks aimed at the more confident rider. There's nothing here really for beginners, but plenty on which more advanced bikers can progress.

You will need to book before your visit; you can either push up or book uplift via the website. Day and evening sessions are available in season, and there is a pop-up cafe on weekends and bank holidays. Full-face helmets and armour are recommended.

Trails

The trails are split into blue, red, black and pro line. However, these are not trail centre blues and competent riders will also find them good fun and a great warm up. As usual in this kind of park, start at a lower grade than you think you ride to warm up and get the feel of the place.

The trails run the length of the hillside, cutting in and out of each other, so it's easy to mix and match and try different variations. It's well worth studying the trail map before you go, or ask for advice when you sign on.

THE DIRT DIRECTORY

While trails are well marked on the hill, it's easy to get slightly confused about which way to go when approaching junctions at speed.

In general, the blues are fast and flowy, with plenty of berms and occasional jumps. The reds have more roots and rocks and bigger jumps – much bigger jumps. The black trails step that up even further, until you have 12-metre tables and gaps on the pro line.

Once you find your way around, you'll find the trails you enjoy and that's a great way to progress your riding.

HAFOD TRAILS

52.0198, -4.0579 / B4337, Nr Llansawel, Carmarthenshire, SA19 7PH / www.hafodtrails.co.uk

New for 2024 and very close to Brechfa, this park is aimed at being family friendly and progressive. It's uplift only so you'll need to book and sign on. There's also the odd enduro race held here too. The trails are still being developed so keep an eye on their socials and website for up-to-date news. It all began so the owners' kids would have somewhere to ride but it's developed quite a long way beyond that with trails between green and black. Some great blue flow trails to warm up on plus some more off-piste-feeling red and black.

BRECHFA

www.mbwales.com/agents/brechfa

ABERGORLECH

51.9843, -4.0592 / Abergorlech, Carmarthenshire, SA32 7SL

BYRGWM

51.9636, -4.1180 / B4310, Carmarthenshire, SA32 7RD

There are two main trail heads for Brechfa which offer a pretty reasonable variety of riding, but make sure you set off from the right trailhead.

Trails
From Abergorlech:
🟥 **Gorlech Trail, 19 kilometres.** There are three big climbs and therefore three big descents on this trail, but it does include a fair amount of fire road work. The trails tends towards the flowy, with some jumps (all rollable) in places. It was designed by Rowan Sorrell, who went on to open BikePark Wales.

From Byrgwm:
🟩 **Derwen Green, 9.2 kilometres.** A very pleasant loop including a good amount (for a green) of easy, rolling singletrack.
🟦 **Derwen Blue, adds 4.7 kilometres to the green.** This loops off the green trail, with slightly more challenging singletrack. It's graded blue more for the distance than the additional difficulty.
⬛ **Raven, 18.5 kilometres.** A good, varied ride with a lot of singletrack, although still some fire road work. There are lots of undulations, twists and fun, if that's your sort of trail.

CWM RHAEADR

52.0648, -3.8025 / Llandovery, Carmarthenshire, SA20 0TL / www.mbwales.com/agents/cwm-rhaeadr

There's only one trail here and it's pretty much a big climb followed by a big descent. The views are pretty good in nice weather.

Trails
🟥 **Cwm Rhaeadr Route, 6.7 kilometres.** There's a long fire road climb to start, and then the final bit of ascent is round some switchbacks. The descent is a winding singletrack with lovely views, with the odd pedally bit thrown in. It's nothing too technical, mostly just flowy, and it's short enough to do laps. Go on a day with good visibility so you can really appreciate the views.

OPPOSITE BRECHFA. © BETHAN LOVERING

CAERSWS BIKE PARK. © MAN DOWN MEDIA

BWLCH NANT YR ARIAN

52.4153, -3.8860 / Ponterwyd, Aberystwyth, Ceredigion, SY23 3AB / *naturalresources.wales/ bwlchnantyrarian*

Bwlch Nant yr Arian offers a great chance to mix and match trails to make a ride as long as you want. There are also running and walking trails and, in season, feeding of the red kites – quite a spectacle. As the name suggests, the forest is at the top of a pass, so on a good day there are stunning views.

Trails

■ **Melindwr, 2 or 5 kilometres.** There are two loops: 2 kilometres for one or 5 kilometres for both. Both loops do include a fair amount of fire road climbing, but the descents are lovely swooping flow trails which are immense fun.

There are several red-graded trails which can be combined in various ways to make as long a ride as you wish.

■ **Pendam, 10 kilometres.** This is the quick blast version of the trails available here, with a mix of fire roads, very quiet road and singletrack. The singletrack tends towards the flowy rather than the technical.

■ **Summit Trail, 18 kilometres.** This trail includes the Pendam trails but adds an extra loop to include the rather fine descent Mark of Zorro; a swoopy singletrack with the odd jump which descends for ages. You'll forgive pretty much any amount of fire road for this.

■ **Syfydrin, 35 kilometres.** This is only black graded because of its length and remoteness. It includes all of the Summit Trail but adds a great chunk of moorland wandering as well. You will need to take adequate supplies and be prepared if you choose this route. It is best done when there is visibility so you can actually see the views.

Other features

There is a skills area with a pump track, a flow trail and a jump line. It is great for sessioning. There are plenty of tables, step-ups and even a wall ride. And while everything is rollable, it's a good place to progress too.

CAERSWS BIKE PARK

52.5360, -3.4540 / Caersws, Powys, SY17 5JE / *caerswsbikepark.co.uk*

An absolutely iconic British DH venue, having been used as a race venue since 2004. It still holds regular rounds of both local and national DH races. The park has been revamped and regular uplift is now available through the website as well as private sessions where you get to play on the hill with just your friends, and there's coaching with ex-pro Matt Simmonds. You will need a full-face helmet and protection to ride.

Trails

There are five trails at the time of writing but there are plans to expand. Two reds and three blacks (definitely not trail centre grading) with cross-over points so you can mix and match on the way down. The trails here are known for being fast, steep and technical – proper DH territory. It can get very claggy and slidey in wet conditions, or incredibly loose if it's dry. Essentially, whatever the weather you'll end up sliding down a steep Welsh hillside.

DYFI BIKE PARK. © MAN DOWN MEDIA

DYFI BIKE PARK

52.6229, -3.8502 / Esgair Forest, Pantperthog, Machynlleth, Powys, SY20 9AS / www.dyfibikepark.co.uk

Once upon a time there were three siblings who were all incredibly handy on bikes. Between them, the Athertons have ridden pretty much every sort of gravity riding there is, so when Dan Atherton designs a bike park you know it's going to be on the gnarly side of things rather than something tame and gentle.

This place is amazing, but it is big, so you need to be a pretty confident rider before coming here. Even the trails described as 'rollable' are on a much bigger scale than pretty much anywhere else. And that's an Atherton definition of 'rollable'. Plus, why are you coming to Dyfi to roll things?

You will need to book and sign a waiver before you go. Full-face helmets and kneepads are mandatory. You may prefer more armour as well. There's a mix of DH-style trails and smoother flow/jump lines. It's best to read trail descriptions before you go (such as the diamond grading system explained below) or ask for advice at the signing-on point. Warm up on something more gentle before hitting the big stuff.

It's an amazing day out if you have the skills.

Trails

■ **Super Swooper, 3.1 kilometres.** This is a big red flow trail, so expect lots of berms and tables. It's fast rolling and smooth for the most part.

Turns in the Ferns, 1 kilometre. This is a shorter red run lower down the mountain, so it is more sheltered. It's more of a varied track than Super Swooper in terms of surface, and with more technical sections.

Lovey Dyfi, 3.6 kilometres. The 'mellower' red trail, although you'll still need to be a confident rider. Emphasis on flow, berms and tables with some optional bigger jumps lower down.

■ **El Hippo, 500 metres.** Another of the tracks lower down the hill. Two big hip jumps give the track its name, plus it has lots of berms and jumps and as well as a technical rooty section.

◆ According to the Athertons, riders can roll anything on these tracks.

50 Hits, 3.7 kilometres. As the name might suggest, this trail is all about the jumps – lots and lots of them. Big jumps, small jumps, hips, boosters, step-ups, step-downs – they are all on this track.

Insta360 – FlowState, 3.6 kilometres. A black mostly flow trail, but also expect rock features, a wall ride (optional) and an unavoidable, definitely not-rollable drop. Fast, flowy and big.

◆ ◆ These tracks have 'obstacles that can't be rolled but we've built alternative lines around the side.'

Original DH, 1.8 kilometres. Accessible from the Race Track, this was the first line built at Dyfi. It's a varied track, like many DH courses, with everything from big berms and jumps to technical sections.

Race Track, 2.8. kilometres. A DH track used by several pros for training, this has a bit of everything you could want to challenge yourself – but you have to be skilled to ride it well.

◆ ◆ ◆ These tracks have 'obstacles that can't be rolled and don't have alternative lines.'

Slab Track, 1.4 kilometres. This is an alternative start to the Race Track. It's steep, loose, very technical and rocky at the top before becoming jumpy.

Oakley – Icon Way, 1 kilometre. This was designed as a pro line jump track. You may spend more time in the air than on the ground.

Fire in the Booth, 400 metres. A triple-black-diamond off-piste trail which starts off quite flowy but then changes to steep, rooty, rocky, very technical gnadgery goodness after the fire road. Expect lines to change with every ride, especially in the wet.

DYFI FOREST

52.6412, -3.8334 / Heulfryn, Machynlleth, Powys, SY20 9HB / *beiciomynydddyfi.org.uk*

Dyfi Forest is absolutely not to be confused with Dyfi Bike Park! This is much more of an old-school trail centre.

The forest is used for the annual Dyfi Enduro event. Also in the area are the three Mach trails from Machynlleth. All are signed on public rights of way and the GPX are available from *beiciomynydddyfi.org.uk*

Trails

■ **ClimachX, 15 kilometres.** There's a chunk of fire road climbing, although there are also some undulating singletrack sections. Indeed, it's not a straight-up-and-down route, but more of a meandering one. The last descent, Tony the Tiger, is a bit more techy, but does have glorious views if you can look at them. It's also one of the longest purpose-built descents in Wales.

OPPOSITE COED Y BRENIN. © *VINCENT GREGORY*

COED Y BRENIN

52.8242, -3.8964 / Ganllwyd, Dolgellau, Gwynedd, LL40 2HZ / *naturalresources.wales/coedybrenin*

COED Y BRENIN. © *ANDY SCARSBROOK*

Coed y Brenin was the first forest to be developed for mountain biking in the UK, but development has continued aplenty since, meaning there's a range of trails suitable for pretty much every rider. The trails can be linked in several ways, which are handily labelled for riders. Development of the blue trail means there is pretty much something for everyone here, plus it's really easy to use the trail maps to devise your own variation, especially if you fancy trying something a bit harder but don't want to commit to the full version.

The whole place is great for biking: there's plenty of historical remains in the area to nosy at, plus tracks and bridleways crossing the entire area. It's also been used for plenty of events over the years. A real slice of MTB trail centre history.

Trails

■ **MinorTaur, up to 12 kilometres.** This comprises several loops of thoughtfully built blue flow trail with some fun trail features. There's a reasonable amount of climbing, so be aware of the effort level for the young and the unfit, but because it's in loops, cutting it short is easy. The furthest loop is mainly fire road, but it is scenic and worth doing. It runs parallel with, and uses, some of the green Yr Afon trail, so you can try bits of the blue without over-committing.

■ **Temtiwr, 8.7 kilometres.** This is a short, 'tempting' loop with some techy ups and downs – expect rocks and roots – but with a big fire road climb in the middle. It's not an easy red, so don't jump straight in from the blue if you are unconfident on techy stuff.

■ **Cyflym Coch, 12.6 kilometres.** Despite starting with a techy climb, this 'fast red' links together the more flowing sections of the red trails, so it's a logical step up from the MinorTaur. This is – kind of – the red flow trail, and if you don't fancy the first techy bit, you can use the blue route along the valley.

■ **Dragon's Back, 31 kilometres.** A big old ride of pretty much all the red trails, but with loops and escape routes should it become too much. There are some long sections of fire road linking some of the singletrack sections on the far loop.

■ **Beast, 35 kilometres.** Another big old ride, but with more technical sections as it includes something from pretty much all the trails at Coed y Brenin, including the black trails. It also uses the long fire road sections on the furthest loop out.

■ **MBR, 18.4 kilometres.** This has a little bit of everything – techy and rocky ups and downs, flowy bits and obviously some fire road climbs. A modern classic.

■ **Tarw Du, 20.2 kilometres.** This trail, the 'Black Bull', pretty much started it all – it's probably the first purpose-built MTB trail in the UK. Without it, this book wouldn't exist. It's on the other side of the road and valley from the other trails. Unfortunately, its age shows in the amount of fire road it involves; this is what trails used to be like, but thankfully we've moved on. The singletrack tends towards the rocky, and Y Slab is a prominent feature.

Multi-use trails

■ **Yr Afon, 10.8 kilometres.** This can be used as an escape route from the blue trail.

Other features

■ **Y Ffowndri skills area** has various features for all levels, including some bigger jumps and drops. It can help to give you an idea about what to expect on the trails.

OPPOSITE COED Y BRENIN. © *ANDY SCARSBROOK*

THE DIRT DIRECTORY

ONE GIANT LEAP DH. © *MAN DOWN MEDIA*

REVOLUTION BIKE PARK

52.8202, -3.4079 / Llangynog, Powys, SY10 0EP / *www.revolutionbikepark.co.uk*

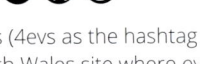

Revs (4evs as the hashtag goes) is another North Wales site where everything is larger than usual. Like Dyfi Bike Park (p111), this is not a place for beginners or the unconfident, but for gnarly riding and big jumps it's got an immense reputation.

Unfortunately, while writing this book Revs received the rather devastating news that part of the wood had a disease called *phytophthora ramorum*, requiring compulsory felling of all the larch trees. This meant the park had to close while the work went on.

However, work is going well. Trees have been taken out and new ones planted, and the tracks that weren't too badly hit have been revamped. This allowed them to open partially for summer 2024 – check their socials for updates (@*revolutionbp* on Instagram). You will still need to book on and wear a minimum of full face and knee pads; all the usual stuff.

Longer term, they'll strive to be even better at providing the gnarly stuff they've always been famed for. Being the sort of people they are, those that run Revs are seeing this as an opportunity to build the new forest around the tracks – the opposite way round from trying to put tracks into an existing forest. So, there are lots of exciting plans ahead – we'll all just have to be patient. #revs4evs

ONE GIANT LEAP DH

52.9563, -3.1473 / Tan-y-graig Farm, Llangollen, Denbighshire, LL20 8AR / *www.onegiantleapllangollen.co.uk*

There are plenty of enduro/gravity-based events held here. If you want to ride outside of these events then you need to be a member and check if the site is open for riding. The Facebook page gives up-to-date info on events and uplifts. Because the start and end of the trails are linked by a public road, you can arrange your own uplift.

Coaching sessions are also available and there is a camping pod at the farm.

Trails

Expect these trails to feel harder than their gradings. This place is aimed at those who like it steep, techy and loose, and all the trails reflect that. There is regular DH and enduro racing on site – which is another way of getting to ride the trails.

The easiest trail is **Gentle Giant** (500 metres), so that is the place to start on your first trip or as a warm-up. It is steep, technical and loose, and also rides very differently in wet and dry conditions. The trails then get steeper, more technical and looser. Put it this way, Bernard Kerr has used the place as a training ground for world cup DH. This is absolutely not a place for the unconfident.

OPPOSITE REVOLUTION BIKE PARK. © *TIM WESTWOOD*

THE DIRT DIRECTORY

COED LLANDEGLA. © JOOLZE DYMOND

COED LLANDEGLA

53.0630, -3.1352 / Ruthin Road, Llandegla, Denbighshire, LL11 3AA / www.oneplanetadventure.com

This is a well-known and popular centre, which has a lot to offer riders with many levels of riding ability. All the trails start with the climb up to the top of the forest. There's no way round this – just tap it out up the long fire road while wishing you were on an ebike. Yes, it does go on forever, but it does end and it means there's a lot of downhill to come. The grades here are pretty soft, so the red trail isn't too bad for those new to reds. There's also running and walking routes here, skills courses, Wednesday night socials and regular events and races. The Offa's Dyke National trail also passes through the forest.

It's worth carrying the trail map with you so you can mix and match trails and session sections.

Trails

■ **12 kilometres.** This shares the first climb with the red trail and then, after a promising hint of singletrack, becomes mostly much broader tracks with few features. It's easy to ride, though not overly exciting after the first couple of sections. From Dusk Til Dawn is a link through to the red trail – it joins it about halfway through if you are finding the blue too easy or want to cut the red trail short.

■ **15 kilometres.** There is the long climb to start, but then it is mostly singletrack of the flowy rather than techy sort. There are berms and rollers and a few drops, but nothing that can't be rolled. There are a few joining fire road sections. This is not a particularly hard red, so it's worth a try if you would like to progress your trail riding. You can use the old blue trail to cut out the final section which does involve a fair chunk of climbing. Mostly, it's a lot of flowy fun.

■ The black sections all come off the red route which at least means you are nicely warmed up and used to the trail conditions before hitting them. Most black entry points have a qualifier – if you can't get over this feature then the rest of the trail isn't for you. They aren't particularly technical black sections – it's mostly flow and jumps of various sizes. Obviously the more confident you are on jumps the more you will get out of the trail, but if you are looking to push your grade, they are a good option. B Line is the jump line, freshly rebuilt in 2024, with a link back to the start so it can be sessioned.

The black **Natural Selection** is the latest trail at Llandegla and has more of an off-piste enduro flavour to it. Steep, rooty tech with various lines. Greasy in the wet.

Other features

■ There is a skills area, pump track and freeride area.

OPPOSITE COED LLANDEGLA. © JOOLZE DYMOND

WALES

ANTUR 'STINIOG. © *VINCENT GREGORY*

ANTUR 'STINIOG. © *MAN DOWN MEDIA*

ANTUR 'STINIOG

53.0069, -3.9420 / Llechwedd Slate Caverns, Blaenau Ffestiniog, Gwynedd, LL41 3NB /
www.anturstiniog.com

The name Antur 'Stiniog translates into English as 'Stiniog adventure', which describes the place pretty well. Bear in mind that the park is on the side of a mountain in slate mining country – expect weather and rocks, and plenty of both. This is an amazing place to get steep and technical.

The park is uplift only, so you will need to book in advance. Private uplift is available for hire outside of opening hours as well.

A full-face helmet is mandatory on black runs, and is recommended on all other trails. Armour and goggles are also recommended.

Trails

There are currently 14 trails, ranging from green to black. Expect gradings to represent a higher standard than at trail centres, i.e. the blacks are very black. Many of the trails lead into one another or offer variations on a theme, so study the map carefully or ask at the sign-on for advice. Warm up on something you think you'll find easy on your first visit, then work your way up through the grades. As ever, check the harder stuff on foot before you send it.

The green and blue trails are all rollable, but do have enough features that you can get air if you have the confidence and skills. The blacks are steep, loose, rocky and technical, and a lot of fun if that's what you like. The reds are somewhere in between, with one being more of a flow/jump line and the other being more rocky and enduro styled. These are not for the nervous.

OPPOSITE ANTUR 'STINIOG. © *VINCENT GREGORY*

THE DIRT DIRECTORY

PENMACHNO. © VINCENT GREGORY

PENMACHNO

53.0320, -3.8110 / Betws-y-Coed, Conwy, LL24 0YP / www.penmachnobiketrails.org.uk

Penmachno is known for being wet, even by Welsh standards. The trails have a special ability to hold water, therefore getting you wet from below as well as above when it's raining. The trails are remote and can be exposed, so be adequately prepared. It's another of the old-school Welsh trail centres with chunks of fire road connecting the singletrack. Not much has been done to it in recent years, so it's more of an XC route.

Trails

■ **Dolen Machno, 19 kilometres.** This comprises a mix of fairly natural-feeling singletrack and linking fire roads. There are some techy ups as well as downs. It's a touch rocky in places, but nothing too gnarly.

■ **Dolen Eryri, 11 kilometres.** This is the continuation of Dolen Machno, or it can be started from **53.0408, -3.8265** where the trails cross the road. It is largely the same as Dolen Machno.

GWYDIR

53.1320, -3.8091 / Llanrwst, Conwy, LL27 0HX / www.mbwales.com/listings/gwydirmawrandbach

Formerly known as the Marin Trail after the first sponsor, this is one of the original, and old-school, Welsh trail centres.

Trails

■ **Gwydir Mawr, 25 kilometres.** This trail has lots of old-school fire road climbing, connecting sections of singletrack which tend towards the rocky and occasionally quite spicy. The final couple of sections feel more modern in style, with lots of drop-offs and faster rooty, rocky sections.

■ **Gwydir Bach, 8.7 kilometres.** This is a shortened route focused on the singletrack nearest the car park, using the fire roads to loop round. There's still lots of climbing, though. This loop does include the more modern-feeling sections and can easily – apart from the stiffness of the climbs – be sessioned.

MARSH TRACKS

53.3095, -3.4971 / Glan Y Morfa Industrial Estate, Marsh Road, Rhyl, Denbighshire, LL18 2AD / www.marshtracks.co.uk

Marsh Tracks has a closed-circuit road track and a national-standard BMX track, as well as the MTB line. The MTB line is open all the time. The focus is really on the road and BMX tracks.

Trails

There are a couple of short trails mainly aimed at jumping. This is more of a local resource than a destination.

OPPOSITE PENMACHNO. © VINCENT GREGORY

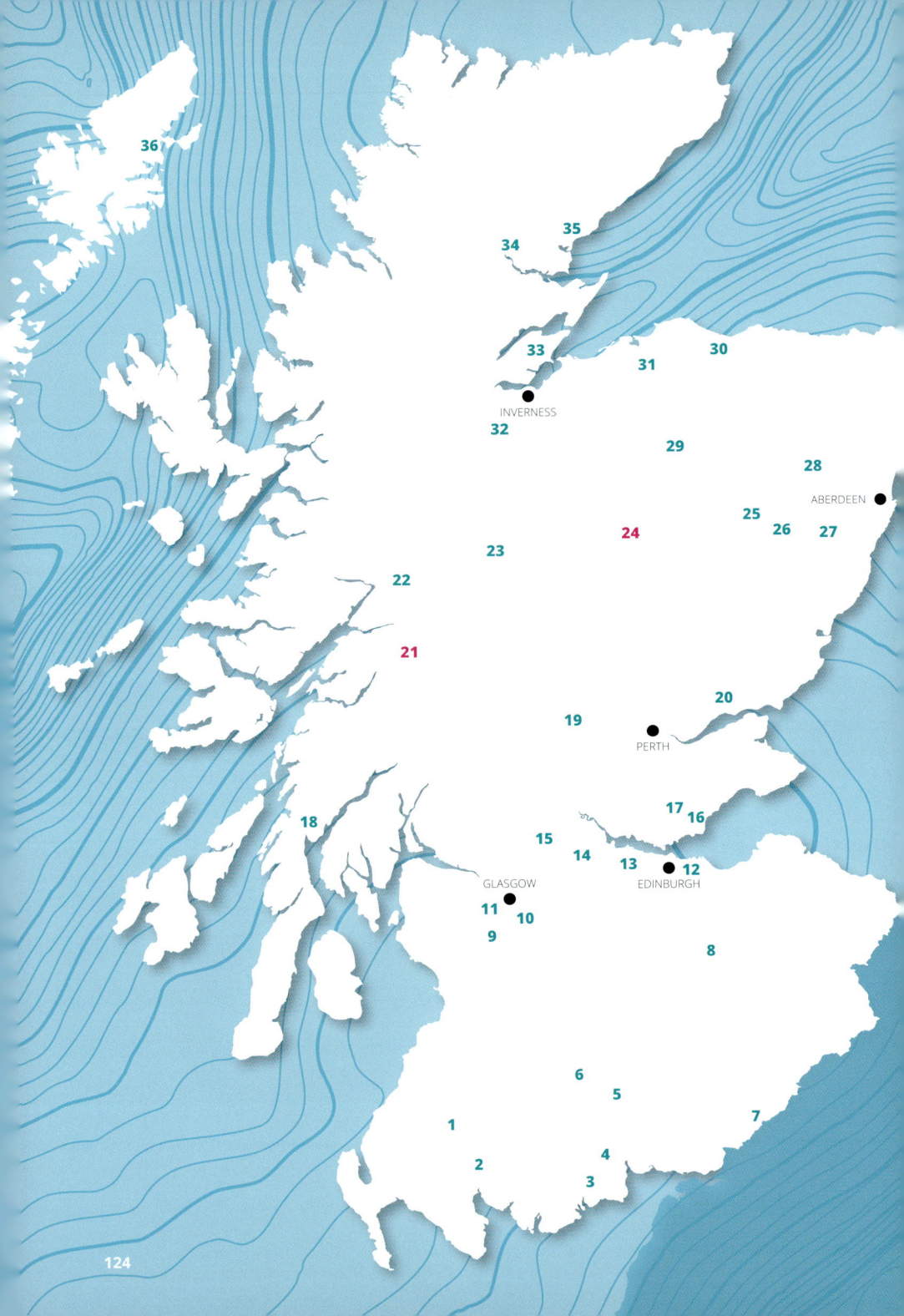

SCOTLAND

Scotland is an utterly amazing place to ride a mountain bike. You are truly spoilt for choice – it has every sort of terrain you could ever wish for, and because of its access laws you are not limited to just bridleways. Remember, where you have rights, you have responsibilities as well: www.outdooraccess-scotland.scot will tell you all you need to know if you are unfamiliar with the enviable Scottish situation.

Developing Mountain Biking in Scotland (*dmbins.com/ride-guide*) has a wealth of resources for ride suggestions that are outside the scope of this book. They also do a huge amount of advocacy, so are well worth supporting. Indeed, advocacy is an area in mountain biking that is very exciting: local agreements and arrangements to allow trails to be built and maintained are much more advanced in Scotland than the rest of the UK, and add massively to the sheer variety of riding. It's little wonder that so many of the UK's top riders, both gravity oriented and XC, have Scottish connections.

If you are wanting a more traditional waymarked route, there are also plenty of those in Scotland. In the early 2000s, Scotland led the way with waymarked routes with the creation of the 7stanes centres in the south, and there's been plenty of development since.

1. Glentrool *p128*
2. Kirroughtree *p128*
3. Dalbeattie *p130*
4. Mabie *p131*
5. Ae *p133*
6. Drumlanrig Castle *p134*
7. Newcastleton *p134*
8. Tweed Valley: Glentress, Innerleithen and the Golfie *p135*
9. Whitelee Windfarm *p138*
10. Cathkin Braes *p139*
11. Pollok Country Park *p139*
12. Skelf Bike Park *p139*
13. Beecraigs Country Park *p139*
14. Callendar Estate *p140*
15. Carron Valley *p140*
16. Middleden Trails *p141*
17. Lochore Meadows Country Park *p141*
18. Achnabreac *p141*
19. Comrie Croft *p143*
20. Templeton Tangle *p143*
21. Glencoe Mountain Resort *p145*
22. Nevis Range *p147*
23. Laggan Wolftrax *p149*
24. Cairngorm Mountain Bike Park *p153*
25. Tarland Trails *p155*
26. Aboyne Bike Park *p157*
27. Banchory *p157*
28. Pitfichie *p157*
29. Glenlivet *p158*
30. Moray Monster Trails *p159*
31. Sanquhar Woodlands *p160*
32. Abriachan Kelpies' Trails *p160*
33. Learnie Red Rocks *p161*
34. Balblair *p162*
35. Golspie – Highland Wildcat *p162*
36. Lews Castle Grounds *p162*

THE DIRT DIRECTORY

COMRIE CROFT. © *COMRIE CROFT*

THE DIRT DIRECTORY

GLENTROOL. © ANDY McCANDLISH

GLENTROOL

55.0748, -4.5515 / Newton Stewart, Dumfries and Galloway, DG8 6SZ (nearest post code) / *forestryandland.gov.scot/visit/forest-parks/galloway-forest-park/glentrool-visitor-centre*

Glentrool is one of the 7stanes, but this one is all about the big, long rides through the hills and valleys of Galloway, rather than the singletrack. And the views; it's always best to do rides here on a clear day, so you can see the scenery. Both National Cycle Network route 7 and the Southern Upland Way connect into Glentrool if you want to make your ride even longer. You can also use the Big Country Route to link into Kirroughtree.

Trails
- **The Glen, 6 kilometres.** This includes some easy singletrack.
- **The Green Torr, 9 kilometres.** This is a longer variant of the green trail. It does include a longish climb, but therefore a longer descent.
- **The Big Country Route, 58 kilometres.** This is all on fire and minor roads, but has plenty of ups and downs. It's an excellent tour of a chunk of Galloway, even if technically undemanding. Take enough supplies with you to cope with remote terrain. Gravel bike friendly?

KIRROUGHTREE

54.9535, -4.4206 / Forest Drive, Newton Stewart, Dumfries and Galloway, DG8 7BE / *forestryandland.gov.scot/visit/forest-parks/galloway-forest-park/kirroughtree-visitor-centre*

Also one of the 7stanes, Kirroughtree is another place with plenty of riding, both waymarked and off-piste. The local club, Galloway Hillbillies, not only organise local riding but also plenty of events, and they are dab hands at building interesting courses. There are enduros, endurance, duathlons and XC events all based here during an average year. In 2022, Kirroughtree hosted the British Cycling National Cross Country Championships, including the first ever short track event, as well as the Scottish MTB XC Championships a few weeks later.

This is where the awesomely talented Scottish rider Rab Wardell won his Scottish Champs title a couple of days before his untimely passing. RIP, Rab, and thank you for all you ever did for MTB.

Trails
- **Bargaly Wood, 6 kilometres.** This is mostly fire roads and quiet roads, but it includes some easy singletrack taking you up a small glen.

OPPOSITE KIRROUGHTREE. © ANDY McCANDLISH

THE DIRT DIRECTORY

DALBEATTIE. © *JOHN COEFIELD*

■ **Larg Hill, 10 kilometres.** This is about half and half fire road and very pleasant singletrack. You can add the Doon Hill extension (4 kilometres), but that adds distance rather than much in the way of singletrack.

■ **The Twister, 17 kilometres.** This is made up of lots of twisty singletrack, which is technical at times in an XC sort of way, both up and down. There are no particularly big features, but it's quite a challenging route physically.

■ **Black Craigs, 14 kilometres.** This comes off the red route, so it's 31 kilometres in total unless you park further up the valley and do it from the far end. There are some shortcuts if it all gets too much. The route involves lots of singletrack with some technical ups and downs. It also includes the amazing glaciated granite slabs of McMoab – there's nothing quite like them. A good, challenging ride.

DALBEATTIE

54.9129, -3.8179 / A710, Dalbeattie, Dumfries and Galloway, DG5 4QU / *forestryandland.gov.scot/visit/dalbeattie*

Dalbeattie is another of the original 7stanes, although it's not had the investment in recent years that some of the others have. However, if you want to get out for a big old XC ride, it's perfect for that. There's nothing much at the trailhead, but the town of Dalbeattie is close by.

Trails

■ **Moyle Hill Trail, 14 kilometres.** This trail comprises some singletrack, but mostly fire roads. This is an old-school blue route which sadly hasn't been updated.

■ **Hardrock Trail, 25 kilometres,** including The Slab which is classed as black. This trail

SCOTLAND

DALBEATTIE. © *JOHN COEFIELD*

is long with lots of fire road, but it can be cut shorter. The Slab is probably the defining feature of the trail, a big, glaciated chunk of granite – if you've not ridden it before, have a quick look at it first. It can be bypassed if it looks too much. There's a second slab feature at The Terrible Twins further along the ride. The singletrack is varied, undulating through woods and more open country. Most technical features are rocky, but there is plenty of easy trail if you just want a long XC ride.

■/■ **Blue Taster Loop, 4 kilometres.** A small loop which is handy to get used to the granite of Dalbeattie, for a quick blast or to practise skills. Or just for a play.

Multi-use trails

■ **Ironhash Trail, 11.5 kilometres.**

MABIE

55.0225, -3.6430 / Dumfries, Dumfries and Galloway, DG2 8HB / *forestryandland.gov.scot/visit/mabie*

Mabie is yet another of the 7stanes, and another that hasn't really been developed since it was first built. This means the blue trail is underwhelming, although the red is pretty good fun. There are also walks and an adventure playground.

Trails

■ **Woodhead Loop, 10 kilometres.** This trail has some singletrack, but not very much – it's mostly fire roads.

■ **The Phoenix Trail, 19 kilometres.** There is a pleasingly high proportion of singletrack to fire road on this trail. It comprises a lot of pretty flowy trail with the odd rocky feature, but nothing too extreme. It also includes the occasional black option. It's good if you are looking to up your grade, and it's also easy just to try smaller sections of trail.

Multi-use trails

■ **Big Views Loop, 8 kilometres.**

Other features

■ **Dirt jump line.** This has doubles and tables, which are all rollable or sendable.
■ **Skills park.** This is pretty small but quite fun, with a few red and blue options.

SCOTLAND

AE. © ANDY McCANDLISH

AE

55.1889, -3.5963 / Ae Village, Dumfries, Dumfries and Galloway, DG1 1QB / *forestryandland.gov.scot/visit/forest-of-ae* / Uplift: *www.adrenalinuplift.co.uk*

The Forest of Ae is one of the original 7stanes and it offers a fair bit of variety, from gentle family routes to more technical riding, plus a lot of off-piste routes. It's well known and loved by the enduro crews; it holds plenty of races with a gravity slant. The trails are either easy fire road tracks or suitable for the already confident, but if you are happy on steepish tracks with a few rocks there is plenty for you.

There are also many off-piste lines in the forest with an enduro feel to them. Expect slithering, steep, rooty goodness.

Trails

■ **Ae Valley Route, 9 kilometres.** This is mostly fire road with a little bit of singletrack. It goes up the valley so stays relatively flat, making it suitable for small legs.

■ **Larch Blue Route, 13.5 kilometres.** This is mostly fire road with a little bit of very easy singletrack; a longer version of the green really, rather than a proper blue trail, with a few more hills added.

■ **Ae Line Trail, 24 kilometres with some black sections.** This track has surprisingly little fire road for a trail of its age. Features can be rolled, but can also be attacked by someone with more confidence. There are quite a few chances to get air. The final descent has been recently rebuilt as a flow trail, and is worth sessioning if it grabs your fancy. The push-up path for the DH lines runs parallel to the lower section of the Omega Man, meaning a play on the jumps before you go back to the car is nice and easy.

■ **The Shredder, 1 kilometre.** This is a 'beginner' DH/enduro line. It's a little bit loose and rocky. There is one large drop that must be sent, or alternatively you can roll round it – check it out on your first run. There are plenty of doubles that can be rolled or jumped. The trail then joins the lower section of the Omega Man, or alternatively you can push straight back up. It's a good introduction to the gnarlier trails at Ae.

■ **Ae Downhill, 1.6 kilometres.** This is a much more serious DH/enduro line – it's steeper, rockier and generally gnarlier than the Shredder, and the gap jumps get larger and more frequent. It's worth a walk before you send.

OPPOSITE AE. © JOOLZE DYMOND

THE DIRT DIRECTORY

DRUMLANRIG CASTLE

55.2747, -3.8097 / Thornhill, Dumfries and Galloway, DG3 4AQ / *www.drumlanrigcastle.co.uk*

MTB trails are maybe not what you might expect at a castle and country estate which is the home of the Duke of Buccleuch and Queensberry, but along with the house and gardens there are some MTB trails and plenty of easier, family oriented riding.

There are tours of the 17th-century castle, the Pink Palace, as well as Victorian gardens and an adventure playground, so a trip here can be made into a family day out.

Trails

🟩 There is a selection of more family oriented trails, ranging from 3–13 kilometres on fire roads through the estate.

🟦 **Copy Cat, 7 kilometres.** This uses fire roads to shadow the second bit of the red trail, hence its name, but dips in and out of the easier red bits. It's great for trying stuff out.

🟥 **The Old School, 10 kilometres for the full loop, 6 kilometres for the shorter loop.** Expect natural-feeling rooty goodness and making the most of the terrain to keep you on your toes (or on the floor). Originally built when 26-inch wheels could get round tight corners.

NEWCASTLETON. © *JOOLZE DYMOND*

NEWCASTLETON

55.1797, -2.8127 / Douglas Square, Newcastleton, Scottish Borders, TD9 0QD / *forestryandland.gov.scot/visit/newcastleton*

Newcastleton is another of the 7stanes centres, and another which hasn't benefitted from investment like some of the others. The trailhead was moved to the village, so at least there are places to eat and get supplies locally, plus toilets and even showers. That does mean a ride to the start of the trail proper though. Rock UK, a charity whose land you pass through, is trying to find the means to add a bit of singletrack through their woods. They are keen to develop trails on their land as an extra to the groups they teach. Within the village community, there is hope of developing more trails in a nearby, non-Forestry and Land Scotland woodland which would add a great deal to riding in the area.

Trails

Everything leads out from the village on a track alongside the river, over a splendid bridge and up the hill to Rock UK. A bit more fire road and another bridge and you come to the skills area and the start of the blue climb.

🟦 **9.7 kilometres.** This includes a great switchback climb through the first bit of forestry and a corresponding descent.

🟥 **23.4 kilometres, including the blue trail.** There are some good bits of singletrack on this trail, but an awful lot of fire road. It is pretty old school in design.

Other features

There is also a skills section owned and maintained by Rock UK, with various lines of ascent and descent.

SCOTLAND

GLENTRESS. © ANDY McCANDLISH

TWEED VALLEY

If you had to pick one area in the UK that represents everything mountain biking is in this country, it might well be the Tweed Valley. It's an area that's really embraced the sport, with local towns catering well for mountain bikers, trail advocacy at amazing levels and an absolute heap of stunning riding. There are two trail centres here – Glentress and Innerleithen, part of the original 7stanes development – but where other trails have stagnated, these two sites have continued to develop. No wonder it's where the world championships for XC and marathon were held in 2023. It's also held so very many enduro races at every level, including world. There are bike festivals in the valley annually and a whole general love and enthusiasm for biking that's hard to beat. So, what's the riding like? This description is split into three main chunks: Glentress, Innerleithen and then the other stuff in the valley, including the Golfie.

GLENTRESS

55.6459, -3.1378 / Peebles, Scottish Borders, EH45 8NB / *forestryandland.gov.scot/visit/forest-parks/tweed-valley-forest-park/glentress* / Trail maintenance: *www.facebook.com/trailfairies* / Uplift: *www.adrenalinuplift.co.uk*

Glentress is one of the best-known trail centres in the UK, and consequently it can be a pretty busy place. It's also got something for most riders, and there are plans for development here and throughout the Tweed Valley. Glentress hosted the XC World Championships in 2023, but the course for that has largely been dismantled. There's now a bit of a split between the old and the new trails, with quite a difference in style between them. Until the building work is complete, expect closures and diversions to be in place.

All trails now start from the bottom of the hill where there are full facilities; there is no longer a car park at Buzzard's Nest.

In general, although the centre can hold water in the wet, it doesn't get overly muddy, so it is suitable for riding all year round – you get wet through, but not clagged up. Careful reading of the trail map will also allow you to chop and change between routes or double back on yourself to reride a bit you enjoyed. There are also some sanctioned off-piste trails in the forest, but these aren't marked or maintained in the same way as the official trails.

Trails

🟩 A pleasant mix of fire roads and some singletrack going into the lower forest past the ponds. Gentler gradients than all the other trails.

🟦 **16 kilometres.** The old blue starts with a long and winding singletrack climb up to Buzzard's Nest and then climbs some more for the full route. However, all that climbing makes for great descending and the trails are of great quality for all riders. After the Good Game descent you can either go straight back to the car park on the fire road or traverse across to the new blue flow trail – the first section of this is underwhelming but it gets much better.

🟥 **18 kilometres.** Takes the same outward climb as the blue to Buzzard's Nest with then more climbing, but again, classic descents including the one and only Spooky Woods, and Super G. There are now choices of how to finish: the original line of Magic Mushroom and Falla Brae; the 'natural' lines of Matrix and Lombard Street; or the new red flow trails of Twitcher and Smells like Tweed Spirit. Sounds complicated? It's clearer on the ground and the trail map. It's also popular just to ride the new red flow trails by heading up the fire road – this is clearly signed. Or just (try to) follow the ebikers sessioning the trails.

⬛ **The Glentress Black Route, 29 kilometres.** This can be linked at various points to other trails. In full, this is a big old ride. It gets up high and can get quite exposed, so make sure you have the supplies to deal with it. There is lots and lots of climbing, but with long descents and plenty of lovely twisting singletrack as well. An epic day out. This also has a new line at the bottom, the style of which is a little different to the rest of the trail.

Other features

🟦/🟥/⬛ **Taster Trails.** The new taster trails are great for warming up on. The idea is if you can ride these happily you'll be fine on the bigger trails. The access trail goes under the *Glentress* sign erected for the Worlds, so it's a great photo op too. The blue has lots of flow, rollers and a short table; the red has bigger features but is still rollable; the black has even bigger features. There's even a short green trail where you'll happily find young ones on balance bikes. Great fun.

INNERLEITHEN

55.6111, -3.0564 / Innerleithen, Scottish Borders, EH44 6PW / *forestryandland.gov. scot/visit/forest-parks/tweed-valley-forest-park/ Innerleithen* / Uplift: *www.adrenalinuplift.co.uk*

While there are no facilities at the trailhead, there are toilets and lots of places to eat and stay in Innerleithen itself, which is an incredibly welcoming biking town – there are bike shops and bike hire in the centre. This is the sort of place where the local cafes sponsor events and riders.

Trails

🟥 **Innerleithen XC, 19 kilometres.** This involves a big old climb up to Minch Moor, but then big descents back down, including some optional black sections. It can be exposed on top, so be prepared. In the main it's fairly straightforward singletrack, and quite a lot of it, with the odd rocky feature. There are more jumps and drop-offs towards the end. The descent will tire you more because of its length than its gnarliness.

🟧 **Innerleithen Downhill.** There are four waymarked trails from Plora Rig down, but there are also several unmarked trails which, because of the local Tweed Valley Trails Association partnership agreements, are sort

OPPOSITE GLENTRESS. © ANDY McCANDLISH

INNERLEITHEN. © *JOHN COEFIELD*

GOLFIE. © *RICHARD BARSON*

of sanctioned. Hence Inners' reputation for the enduro and DH lovers. There is lots to have a go at here: expect steep, rugged, twisting, gnarly stuff – this is not XC territory, and it's probably wise to visit in a full-face helmet and protection. Be sure to check the individual trail gradings before you launch into something beyond your skill level, and check with locals about the unmarked stuff. You can ride/push up or book uplift.

Other stuff

The hard work from the Tweed Valley Trails Association, liaising with Forestry and Land Scotland and other landowners, plus the actual work to develop the trails, means that the trails in Caberston Forest, better known as the Golfie, are kept maintained. They are not waymarked but they are on Trailforks or you can ask locally in the valley for suggestions. There's a lot of steep, sketchy, natural-feeling awesome stuff here, perfect for enduro gnarr shredding. This is not XC territory, however, and it's not for the beginner.

Park in Innerleithen for the Golfie and make your way into the forest on the various fire roads available for ascent, depending on which trails you fancy. It's going to be a long way up, but that just means the descents are long too.

Between Inners and the Golfie there are plenty of enduro events, ranging from local level to world-class standard.

Because the Tweed Valley is so popular, not just for mountain biking but also for walking and horse riding, Forestry and Land Scotland have come up with a zoning plan of the forests to try to ensure all user groups have a good day out without conflict. That means there are certain areas where mountain bikers are not encouraged. Please respect that agreement – there is enough amazing riding in the Tweed Valley already. There's more info on the F&LS web page for Innerleithen.

WHITELEE WINDFARM

55.7101, -4.3320 / Moor Road, Eaglesham, East Renfrewshire, G76 0QQ / www.eastrenfrewshire.gov.uk/cycling-at-whitelee

It can be windy at Whitelee Windfarm, but that's sort of the point as it's the site of the UK's largest onshore windfarm. There's a visitor centre introducing the site and the concept of wind power, and you can even take a bus tour around some of the turbines. Or, you can ride round all of them, which is about 160 kilometres. It's an area more suited to gravel riding on the forest roads, which isn't overly exciting for mountain bikers, but it's interesting to see turbines up close and personal.

Trails

■ With red sections. There is a short dedicated trail.

SCOTLAND

CATHKIN BRAES

55.8010, -4.2223 (Parking at **55.8012, -4.2223** and **55.7945, -4.2179**) / Cathkin Road, Glasgow, G45 0HR / *glasgow.gov.uk/article/4174/Cathkin-Braes-Country-Park-and-Local-Nature-Reserve*

Cathkin Braes is the legacy from the 2014 Commonwealth Games which were held in Glasgow, with some extra bits added since, such as for the Glasgow 2018 European Championships. It's still used for regional and national racing. It is quite a compact site, so none of the trails are very long, but that does mean they can be easily sessioned. It's really a case of exploring and finding your favourite bits, and because it still gets used for racing you will find new bits popping up here and there.

There are also off-piste trails in the park, but it gets busy, so be aware of other users.

Trails

- **Flow track.** This is fun and flowy, but short.
- **Blue Circuit, approximately 5.5 kilometres.** This 'old blue' takes you around the park and up and down. It's pretty XC in feel, and does have some more interesting sections popping off it.
- **European XC course.** This does include some more interesting features which, again, can be sessioned.

Other features

There is a pump track, which is world-class standard and so much fun.

There are varying difficulties on a jump line short enough to be sessioned. The jumps can be rolled or sent.

There is also a short dual slalom track for sorting out arguments between friends.

POLLOK COUNTRY PARK

55.8287, -4.3179 / Bellahouston, Glasgow, G43 1AT / *www.glasgow.gov.uk/pollokcountrypark*

Pollok Country Park has some short, undemanding trails within its grounds. This is a busy park, so be aware of other users.

Trails

- 500 metres.
- 1 kilometre.
- 1.3 kilometres.

These are very short circuits, but they can be joined together to make a longer ride. They are not particularly technical, but are pleasant off-road riding.

SKELF BIKE PARK

55.9449, -3.1788 / Bowmont Place, Edinburgh, EH8 9RY

Nestling under the west side of Arthur's Seat, there's a great pump track and a very short blue trail.

BEECRAIGS COUNTRY PARK

55.9497, -3.6053 / Linlithgow, West Lothian, EH49 6PL / *www.facebook.com/BeecraigsMTB-trails* / *www.westlothian.gov.uk/beecraigs*

A mix of trails within a busy and popular country park. Some trails are shared, so be aware of other users. There are also some dedicated MTB trails to suit most users.

- **3.6 kilometres.** Mostly on shared fire roads.
- **5.3 kilometres.** Follows most of the green route but with some additional easy singletrack.
- **7 kilometres.** Two loops in a sort of figure-of-eight shape with some optional black sections. Expect roots and mud when wet, and fire roads to link the good bits.

There's also a skills park and small jump line, plus additional local trails in the woods.

Within a few miles are several urban pump tracks – Fraser Park, Craigspark in Livingston, Bridgend Park – small but good local tracks.

THE DIRT DIRECTORY

INNERLEITHEN. © ANDY McCANDLISH

CALLENDAR ESTATE

55.9867, -3.8271 / Lochgreen Road, Falkirk, FK1 3AZ / *www.callendarestate.co.uk/activities/cycling*

The Callendar Estate has short trails with an XC flow feel to them. They're great for beginners or unconfident riders, and there's nice progression between the grades. There are some off-piste trails as well. There's nothing here really for the gnarr seeker, and the grades are pretty soft, but it's a good local facility for Falkirk – it's playing in the woods on bikes in a slightly more structured way.

Trails

🟩 **Canada Trail, 4.1 kilometres.** This involves gentle ups and downs, and it's well-surfaced and straightforward.

🟦 **Craigieburn Trail, 3.4 kilometres.** This is slightly more challenging than the green trail, with a few more undulations.

🟧 **Auchingean Trail, 7.5 kilometres.** This is an extension to Craigieburn Trail further into the woodland. There are a few berms and tables here, all rollable, which are good for developing skills. There are also a few off-piste lines which tend to be more natural feeling, with mud and slippery roots in wet conditions. The wood is quite small, so you can't really get lost if you go exploring.

🟥 **Kilbean Trail, 2.3 kilometres.** This can be connected to the other trails using the John Muir Way, or you can park closer. It's a good option for extending the ride and having a bit more fun.

CARRON VALLEY

56.0304, -4.0534 / B818, Denny, Falkirk, FK6 5JL / *forestryandland.gov.scot/visit/carron-valley*

There is only one trail here, although there's a walking trail along the side of the reservoir,

140

fishing and a replica medieval village open to the public on occasion. Depending on where you live, it's a perfect place for an after-work blast.

Trails

 8 kilometres. This is a fairly soft-graded red route: all the features are rollable or avoidable. It's got more of a flowy XC feel. The trail is a mix of fire road and trail climbing, and then three sections of (mostly) descent with connecting fire road. It's a good red route if you are looking to try the grade.

There are also unmarked trails up Harran and Benarty hills behind the park which are good fun.

Trails

🟢 **6 kilometres.** This goes around the loch and is suitable for all beginners.

🔵 **5 kilometres.** There is nothing too techy on this trail, but it's quite fun, with berms and rollers.

 500 metres. A short section in White Wood with some slightly harder challenges.

MIDDLEDEN TRAILS

56.1316, -3.1641 / Dunnikier Way, Kirkcaldy, Fife, KY1 3LR

🅿️

This site might be small but it's a great introduction to easier trails. A great little local facility.

The local Middleden Mountain Bike Club runs skills sessions for kids in the summer.

Trails

Around 5 kilometres in total of mixed green, blue and red trails.

Other features

There is an orange-grade jump park and a pump track.

LOCHORE MEADOWS COUNTRY PARK

56.1504, -3.3366 / Lochgelly, Fife, KY5 8BA / *www.lochoremeadows.org/activity-listing/cycling*

This is a great local facility for encouraging cycling, and there is a track around the lake suitable for all bikes including adaptive cycles. There's also a chance to hire adaptive bikes and be shown how to use them at the activity centre.

ACHNABREAC

56.0626, -5.4524 / Lochgilphead, Argyll and Bute, PA31 8RE / *forestryandland.gov.scot/visit/achnabreac*

🅿️

Set in the historically very important kingdom of Dalriada (the fort is close by), most people come here to explore the huge amount of prehistoric remains in the local area. Kilmartin has a museum devoted to the subject if you are at all interested in prehistoric and early medieval Scotland. There's also plenty of local riding of the pottering-about-pleasantly sort, such as the Crinan Canal.

Trails

🟧 **Firetower Trail, 14 kilometres.** This is mostly a fire road climb to the old fire tower, where, on a good day, there are cracking views. Then you'll find undulating sections of singletrack back down with optional black sections. There are a few technical features but nothing that can't be rolled, plus there's the opportunity to see prehistoric rock art. On a wet day, the feature called 'Water Splash' can be quite a deep little ford – it can be bypassed using the fire road. This trail is slightly old school, and is of the 'fire-road-linking-singletrack' design.

SCOTLAND

COMRIE CROFT. ALL PHOTOS © *COMRIE CROFT*

COMRIE CROFT

56.3848, -3.9414 / Braincroft, Crieff, Perth and Kinross, PH7 4JZ / www.comriecroftbikes.co.uk

Comrie Croft reckon they have something for everyone – they are quite possibly right. It's got a great variety of trails, from the flowy to the technical. It's been used for regional racing of both XC and gravity flavours (this might just be why Scottish XC riders are so good technically). They are also constantly tweaking and maintaining trails, plus adding new stuff, so check when you get there what the latest routes are. Volunteers are always welcome to help out with trail maintenance.

Trails

The trails here are not particularly groomed; they have more of a natural feel, with plenty of features.

Basically, it's a bit like a bike park in that there are several descent trails of varying grades from blue through to black, which you can mix and match as you please. The climb (not always just upwards) is a mix of fire road and singletrack, leading off to the start of the various descents (not always just downwards). This does allow for progression in your riding, as you can try shorter chunks of trail. Expect a fair bit of rock and roughness – hardtail riders, be warned. If you like technical riding where thoughtful line choice is crucial, this is the place for you.

They also have plenty of suggestions for other riding nearby – MTB, gravel and road riding are all great around here.

TEMPLETON TANGLE

56.4960, -3.0426 / Green Circle, Dundee, DD3 0QG / www.dundeecity.gov.uk/outdoor-access-in-dundee/dundee-mountain-bike-trails

■ **3.2 kilometres.** Short but pleasant trail through the local woods. There's an additional red section which has some rollable, slightly trickier features.

143

SCOTLAND

GLENCOE MOUNTAIN RESORT

56.6320, -4.8280 / Kingshouse, Glencoe, Highland, PH49 4HZ /
www.glencoemountain.co.uk

GLENCOE MOUNTAIN RESORT. © MAN DOWN MEDIA

Glencoe Mountain Resort is a ski resort in winter and offers other sports during summer, including mountain biking. There is chairlift access to a spicy red and a gnarly black descent, plus some XC trails on the plateau. There are trails at the top of the chairlift (obviously, you'll need to buy a lift pass), but bear in mind these are shared access, although it's not likely to be very busy. It's best to wear protection and a full-face helmet on the downhill runs, given how many rocks there are.

The British National Downhill Championship have been held here in weather so Scottish the event nearly had to be cancelled – be aware that because the bottom of the site is 360 metres above sea level and then the lift takes you up another 400 metres or so, it really can get wild up here. On a clear day, though, the views are stunning.

Trails
XC Trails

There are three marked XC routes in the corrie and on the plateau. These are more waymarked ribbons of singletrack than curated bike park trails so it depends what you are used to. Bear in mind you've just been deposited halfway up a Munro so quite often there will be Scottish weather to ride in, and it's likely to be wet under wheel as well. If you have an accident you are relatively remote so please be prepared.

■ **Nae Danger, 1.5 kilometres.** Uses the fire road to gain a bit more height than the chairlift then wiggles a way round the corrie on the clearest of the three trails.

■ **Epic Glades, 3 kilometres.** Fire road climb and then an undulating route on thin trails around the corrie. It's a fairly natural trail so expect soggy wheel-grabbing sections as well.

■ **Loop du Dhubh, 700 metres.** An extension off the red route to gain a bit more height up Creagh Dhubh so you have a more testing descent.

You can then descend back to the bottom of the hill using the DH trails or there is a fire road.

DH Trails

As you get off the chairlift there's a 250-metre red trail leading to the fire road where the red and black trails proper start. Unfortunately, you do lose quite a bit of height on the fire road before getting to the red.

■ **1 kilometre.** This is steep and techy in places and loose when dry, but it is actually all rollable with avoidable features. It's quite rocky, so full suspension will make life easier and more comfortable. The trail is jumpier down the bottom, but the jumps can be rolled or sent.

■ **900 metres.** This starts with the same link road as the red but comes off the fire road much earlier. It has been called the hardest black in the UK. Warranted? That depends on your riding preferences. Expect rocks and more rocks, drops, steps and having to think about your line very carefully. It's certainly towards the upper edge of trails open to the public; however much travel your bike has, you'll be using it. This is a very tough trail – do not underestimate it. It's quite a chunk harder than the red.

OPPOSITE COMRIE CROFT. © COMRIE CROFT

SCOTLAND

NEVIS RANGE. © *PAUL MASSON*

NEVIS RANGE

56.8522, -4.9985 / Torlundy, Fort William, Highland, PH33 6SQ / *www.nevisrange.co.uk*

Nevis Range is famous for being the home of the UK's only world-cup-standard DH track, and therefore it's the only chance you have in this country of seeing how your skills match up against the world's fastest gravity riders. It's also home to the classic endurance race of 10 Under the Ben – 10-mile laps for 10 hours. It's a busy place for racing – domestic DH and enduros are held here too.

Because it's on the side of a mountain, expect a lot of up to go with your down, whether that's in the gondola or under your own power. It also catches plenty of weather – you only have to look at past photos from DH world cups to see just how much. But on a clear day the views are stunning, especially of the north face of Ben Nevis. I did once stop in a 24-hour race to watch the sun rising over Ben Nevis because it was so spectacular.

The trails are split between those you can ride from the car park and those which require the gondola. There is also a seasonal bike shop and bike hire here too.

Trails
Lower Forest Trails:
Directly from the car park there's a mixture of trails of differing ages and therefore styles.

■ **Blue Adder, 3.4 kilometres.** A lovely flowy, fun blue. There's about a 2-kilometre climb, which is nicely graded, and then a choice of two descents – Voodoo and Blue Adder Descent. It makes a short, easily sessionable loop.

■ **The Witch's World Champs, 8.5 kilometres.** This route has a mix of fire roads and reasonably techy singletrack, with a lot of ascent. It's one of the older tracks here, having been built for the 2007 World Championships.

■ **Wild Goat, 640 metres.** At the bottom of Top Chief (overleaf) is a red trail to take you back down to the car park, but you can ride this separately using fire roads to climb up to the start. It's a fast flow trail, swooping through the trees. A complete contrast and a bit of a rest if you've just come down Top Chief.

■ **Black Crane, 450 metres.** On the steeper and techier side of the trails here – you'll need to access it via the fire road climb that's also part of the World Championship route.

■ **One Dot, 645 metres.** You can use One Dot for the final descent of Top Chief or ride it separately using fire road access. This is the jump line – they start small and end up bigger, although everything is rollable.

OPPOSITE NEVIS RANGE. © *JOHN COEFIELD*

THE DIRT DIRECTORY

NEVIS RANGE. © *JOHN COEFIELD*

From the Gondola:
These routes are just the downs, with gondola uplift to get you and your bike to the top of the hill. Obviously, the gondola stops running if it's too windy. On days where the weather is clear, all these trails come with amazing views. Just concentrate on the trail, though.

■ **Blue Doon, 5.4 kilometres.** This is the newest of the gondola-accessed tracks, and the one with the easiest rating. Beware of some of the flat corners, though, which can't necessarily be ridden as fast as you like, although it's expected maintenance to the trail will tackle these. This trail tends to be loose, especially in dry weather. The top part is exposed hillside, so be prepared for wind; it gets more sheltered and grippier once you are in the woods. This trail suffered badly from storm damage in early 2024, and the proposed repairs include a different line off the hill for the bottom section.

■ **Top Chief, 3.6 kilometres.** This needs confidence and commitment to ride it. It includes a boardwalk section along the side of the hill, plus rocks. Lots of rocks – drops, slabs, smooth rocks, rough rocks, tyre grabbers, all of the rocks. It's sensible, and usual, to pad up. It's a long way down and it's fairly unrelenting so expect to feel battered. The lower section is smoother and flowier with only the odd rock chucked in to test you are still concentrating. One to test both you and your bike. Incidentally, you can cut across to the blue if you feel you have over-committed, as one short section of track is shared. It used to be graded red but now it's black, which gives you a further insight into the standard. And because it's on the side of a mountain it catches the weather – be prepared.

■ **The World Cup DH, 2.8 kilometres.** This is exactly what it suggests. It can be ridden by the very competent and confident normal rider of an enduro persuasion – there are some chicken lines around some of the more terrifying sections. Put it this way – it takes the best in the world nearly five minutes to get down it on full DH rigs. It's known as a very physical and battering track, but it's an absolutely iconic course and there are few places where you can claim to have ridden the same track as the world cup folk. Just don't underestimate it.

Other features
There is also a skills track, a pump track and an orange-grade 4X track which used to hold world-level events. The woods contain some decent off-piste riding too.

SCOTLAND

LAGGAN WOLFTRAX. © PAUL MASSON

LAGGAN WOLFTRAX

57.0003, -4.3169 / A86, Laggan, Highland, PH20 1BU / *forestryandland.gov.scot/visit/laggan-wolftrax*

Laggan Wolftrax was known for being quite challenging but new trails built in 2023 mean it's now got some more friendly and approachable blue trails as part of the offering. There's still the challenging reds and black for those that desire a gnarly day out – wear appropriate armour for these – they are challenging for their grades.

Nearby there is what's known as Laggan Brown, the natural, enduro side with lots of off-piste gnarliness.

Trails

■ **Wolf Cub, 3.5 kilometres.** This has easy gradients and includes some singletrack so is good for kids or as a warm-up.

The blue trails here are designed to be nicely progressive so you can build yourself up to harder trails quite easily. They're also designed to be neatly sessionable – use the blue climb to access the Pict partway up the hill or climb further for Slabba-Dabba-Doo and your first taste of rock.

■ **Blaeberry Flapjack, 400 metres.** The easiest of the blues so the one to try if you are a bit unsure. Starts off the middle fire road and leads down to the Wolf Cub green to take you to the bottom of the hill.

■ **Slabba-Dabba-Doo, 525 metres.** The easiest of the rocky trails at Laggan, so a great one to get your eye in. Everything here

SCOTLAND

LAGGAN WOLFTRAX. © PAUL MASSON

is rollable. Once you've got used to this trail there's a red-graded lead-in trail called Bamm Bamm from slightly further up the hill to add a little extra spice.

■ **The Pict, 300 metres.** The bottom section of Slabba-Dabba-Doo which is smooth and fast flowing. You can also access this directly from partway up the blue climb.

■ **Give and Take, 850 metres.** This is the new blue climb (previously a red descent hence the name) leading to the Lair. You use the fire road to get to the start of the climb but it's then a nice way to gain height. From the Lair you can take your pick of descents, red or blue, or continue ascending on fire roads up to the longer reds.

■ **Howlin' Wolf Red, 800 metres.** Use the link from the Lair to access this fast, flowy, bermy trail with the odd jump. This leads to the lower half of the trail across the fire road.

■ **Leapin' Wolf Red, 700 metres.** More of the same but bigger and more frequent jumps which can be rolled or sent.

■ **Rib Rattler Red and Spare Rib, 2.5 kilometres.** Climb to the Lair and then continue up. This is where it starts to get rocky in the way Laggan is (in)famous for. Bit of a clue in the title. It's good to be padded up. Narrow, nadgy, rocky singletrack with the black option of Air's Rock. The full descent leads back down to the fire road so you can easily repeat. Not an easy red.

■ **Alpha Red, 3.8 kilometres.** Starts off the fire road climb with a bit of technical singletrack climbing before the descent. Then it's fast and techy, lots of rocks. Again, not an easy red. Hardtail riders beware. Protection is wise.

■ **Wolf of Badenoch, 3.9 kilometres.** This comes off the Alpha Red after the climb. It includes lots of rocks and steep, rocky, technical features. Just wear protection. It's reckoned to be one of the hardest blacks at any UK trail centre, and is pretty brutal on the body, much like the original Wolf of Badenoch.

OPPOSITE LAGGAN WOLFTRAX. © PAUL MASSON

SCOTLAND

CAIRNGORM MOUNTAIN BIKE PARK. ALL PHOTOS © PAUL MASSON

CAIRNGORM MOUNTAIN BIKE PARK

57.1334, -3.6706 / Cairngorm Ski Area, Aviemore, Highland, PH22 1RB /
www.cairngormmountain.co.uk/mountain-biking

Built as a summer addition to the winter sports, the Cairngorm trails are very flow based and aimed at the beginner to intermediate riding market. You will need to buy either a half or full day's pass to ride the trails and they are only open during the day – check the website for times. The hillside is split into three zones so go as far up as you like and then ride down. There are plans for further development.

The lower zone is accessed by the conveyor lifts; great for saving little or unfit legs. For the middle and upper zones, you'll have to ride or push up the dedicated tracks – it's just over a kilometre of riding to the top.

Trails

■ **Blaeberry Bumblebee, 180 metres.** Very straightforward flowing green trail suitable for pretty much everyone. Accessed from the top of the upper conveyor. Ends at the bottom of the upper conveyor so you can easily session this as many times as you like.

■ **Golden Dragonfly, 120 metres.** Still very green and flowy but has a couple of rollers to start building you up for the blues.

■ **Hairy Caterpillar 160 metres.** The lower part of the lower zone, accessed from the top of the lower conveyor. Similar to Blaeberry Bumblebee, and a logical continuation, but slightly steeper and faster.

■ **Vole Valley, 250 metres.** Starts from the top of the upper conveyor and is the more straightforward of the blues. It's also the bottom section of the full blue trail so be aware of riders coming down. Keeps the flowy feel but the features are a little bigger. There are a couple of jumps which are rollable or sendable, and some bigger berms.

■ **Stoatally Awesome, 760 metres.** From the very top, expect lots of flow, bigger berms and jumps, and a couple of red alternatives. It does catch the wind, though. All jumps are rollable or sendable.

■ **Weasel Mayhem, 350 metres.** The middle section of the blue with lots of berms. Fast and flowy.

■ **Wobbly Wagtail, 110 metres.** The top red is an alternative to the blue and has tighter berms and a few rocks drops.

■ **Ouzels Delight, 200 metres.** This is the bigger jump line alternative in the middle zone and does include a gap that's not rollable, a pretty big table and then a choice of jumps as you rejoin the blue. Again, easy to session.

SCOTLAND

TARLAND TRAILS. © ANDY McCANDLISH

TARLAND TRAILS. © ANDY McCANDLISH

TARLAND TRAILS

DRUMMY WOODS

57.1264, -2.8658 / Burnside Road, Tarland, Aberdeenshire, AB34 4UP / www.tarland-trails.com

The original Tarland Trails are three short trails accessed from a 650-metre-long fire road. It's simply a matter of riding up the fire road and then choosing the descent of your choice. It's a great small facility for playing and improving your skills, and there is a cafe in the village for afterwards.

Trails
■ **The Spikey Hedgehog, 900 metres.** This is fun and flowy singletrack with a few rollers and berms.
■ **The Red Squirrel, 600 metres.** This comprises singletrack with added rock features, rollers and the odd small drop. Some of the rock features are quite tricky for beginners, so are a chance to improve.
■ **The Slinky Fox jump line, 600 metres.** This features more rollers and then some larger tabletops. Everything can be rolled or sent.

Other features
There's also a pump track.

PITTENDERICH

57.1374, -2.8492 / B9119, Tarland, Aberdeenshire, AB34 4TB / www.tarland-trails.com

The new Tarland Trails – nicknamed TT2 – are located north of the village and are the result of £750,000 of investment. The result? Over a dozen mainly blue and red-grade trails (there's one black) with an emphasis on flow. (If you want tech, there's plenty of local off-piste stuff.) It's well worth studying the trail map on the website and at the trailhead to see how best to get to the bits you want. There's a dedicated way up using a mix of new trail and fire road which leads to the starts of the various trails, or, if you don't want to go right to the top, lead off to the trails partway up. And when you've got to the top there are clear ways to loop back round to session whichever trail takes your fancy. Cleverly designed and well thought out. There are further plans, and all the car parking money goes straight back into the trails.

Trails
■ **Scalextric, 860 metres.** The topmost blue which then leads into the others all the way back down the hill. Fast and flowy, and a whole lot of fun. Includes the odd roller which can be rolled or sent. Crosses a fire road which means you can pedal back round for another go, or head straight down into …

OPPOSITE TARLAND TRAILS. © ANDY McCANDLISH

THE DIRT DIRECTORY

TARLAND TRAILS. © ANDY McCANDLISH

■ **Tomnaverie Turns, 215 metres.** Lots of fast turns including the biggest berm at Tarland.

■ **Holy Cow, 980 metres.** Can be ridden as a continuation of the top blues or accessed by cutting across from the up trail. Still fast flowing but with the addition of a few kickers and drop-offs which also have a ride-around line.

■ **Party Time, 555 metres.** More of the same including kickers and drop-offs. Again, can be ridden as part of the whole or by itself if time is short or weather grim.

■ **Snakes, 700 metres.** A slightly more mellow trail to finish on, or easily sessioned from the parallel climb, **Ladders**. Great trail to start on if you're not sure what to expect.

■ **Crowd surfin', 815 metres.** The blue jump line. Fast and thrilling with tables, berms and kickers all the way down.

The red trails are all further up the hill so will require more initial climbing. The good news is that there are ways back round to the start of all the reds without riding all the way down to the car park.

■ **High Pressure, 1.5 kilometres.** So called because it's best to ride it in a high pressure – not only so you can see the spectacular views, but so you aren't blown off your bike in high winds. Be aware it is 500 metres up an exposed hillside so be prepared with your supplies. Once you've got the weather you've got a cracking swoopy trail with some pedally sections. There's one gap jump – Butt Craic – which has a line round it. At the end of HP you can either continue down the hill on Bermuda and Bon Gripper or cut across to Call me Chris.

■ **Bermuda, 660 metres.** Continuation of High Pressure or can be accessed from the climb. Tight and twisting through the trees so usually more sheltered than High Pressure.

■ **Bon Gripper, 540 metres.** Continuation of Bermuda but back out of the tree line for more flow, the odd rollable drop and bermy fun. Continue to the Spine or head back up.

■ **Spine, 540 metres.** Slightly steeper and with a few straightforward rock gardens. Finishes at the top of the blues or you can use the fire road to go back up and round again.

■ **Call me Chris, 760 metres.** From the top of Pittenderich, again it's fast and flowy with a few rock gardens and alternative lines, swooping berms, and a few rollable jumps. There's also an easy way back up to the top for another go.

■ **Chris Cross, 805 metres.** Continuation of Call me Chris but slightly more flowy. A few rollable jumps and easy rock gardens to add to the mix.

■ **Fool's Gold, 725 metres.** The black jump line with a lot of features. Steady away the first time and then start doubling up. Most features can be taken at a moderate speed but that's not really the point. As ever, there's a trail to take you back round for another run.

ABOYNE BIKE PARK

57.0723, -2.7383 / Bell Wood, Aboyne, Aberdeenshire, AB34 5BJ / www.facebook.com/AboyneBikePark

Park in Aboyne and then follow Low Road along the Tarland Burn towards the water treatment works. Cross the bridge into the wood and follow the trail up to the bike park. It's more of a skills park than anything larger, but it does have opportunities for improving skills at all levels. Volunteers are always welcome to help out with trail maintenance.

This is essentially a slightly more structured version of messing about in the woods on your bike. It's a great little resource, and it's near enough to the Tarland Trails to pay a visit to both in the same day.

Trails
This bike park has three jump lines and a very tiny red trail.

Other features
There's also a pump track.

BANCHORY

57.0589, -2.5253 / Corsee Woods, Banchory, Aberdeenshire AB31 5SA / deesidebikecollective.co.uk

There are three short trails in a small woodland with a fire road climb accessing the top of all three, so brilliant for sessioning.

■ **Dee Lite, 600 metres.** Fast and flowy with jumps, all of which are rollable, or there's stuff you can gap depending on your skill level. The idea is to start with this trail and then work your way up.

■ **Dee Send, 500 metres.** The jumps get bigger and kickier, plus there's a few rock features. Still fast and flowy.

■ **Dee Line, 400 metres.** Bigger jumps still, although nothing too massive, plus bigger rock features.

PITFICHIE

57.2396, -2.5464 (Pitfichie Downhill car park) or 57.2083, -2.5726 (Pitfichie Forest car park) / Inverurie, Aberdeenshire, AB51 7JJ / forestryand-land.gov.scot/visit/pitfichie

Pitfichie is a forest definitely catering for those who like the gnarlier side of life. It's not for those wanting a gentle day out. The granite of Pitfichie adds a lot of spice to all the trails – knee pads at least are probably worthwhile. While there is currently only one waymarked trail, there's plenty of off-piste action as well. Climbing is mostly done on fire roads, waymarked as the Cairn William Trail.

There are regular DH and enduro races held here, and it has been home to the Scottish National MTB DH Championships.

Trails
■ **Granite Top Trail, 6.4 kilometres.** This goes up the fire road to pick up the singletrack climb to the top of Cairn William itself. The Devil's Staircase then heads down. Expect swooping singletrack with rocky sections of both slabs of bedrock and rock gardens. This is a rough trail on a hardtail. You can then use the ascent to loop back round for another bash.

Other features
There are also several unmarked trails leaning towards the steep and techy side, which have been used for enduros. *www.aberdeenshiretrail.org/trails* gives details of the trails which have been adopted and are therefore maintained.

THE DIRT DIRECTORY

GLENLIVET

57.2866, -3.3967 / Ballindalloch, Moray, AB37 9AR / www.bikeglenlivet.co.uk

The 23,000-hectare Glenlivet Estate is part of Crown Estate Scotland, but there has been settlement and farming here since prehistoric times. There are plenty of walking trails as well as MTB, plus fishing, horse riding, a zip wire, a seasonal cafe and a distillery. There are also plenty of historical and scenic sites to visit locally. There's a pretty good variety of trails on the bike site, which should cover most styles of riding.

From the very top of the hill at Carn Daimh are two hand-cut black descents, Daimh Hard and Glenduro, with much more of a natural enduro feel to them.

Trails

■ **Original Blue Loop, 9 kilometres.** This is an XC sort of trail – expect lots of flow and fun. There's a reasonable chunk of climbing for its length, but that means a reasonable amount of descending too.

■ **Bazza's Berms Loop, 5.5 kilometres.** Close to the car park is a flowy blue descent which can be ridden as gently or as hard as you want. It's designed to be sessioned. Or you can include it as part of a longer loop suggested as a more challenging blue ride.

SCOTLAND

GLENLIVET. ALL PHOTOS © *PAUL MASSON*

■ **Red Loop 22 kilometres.** After this comes off the blue trail there's a big old climb, but not only are there glorious views from the top, there's 6.5 kilometres of flowy descent. There are also a few technical features to watch for, with some optional black sections. Some of the trails are hand-cut, so expect roots and more gnarly terrain. The trail can feel exposed at the top in windy conditions. It joins back on to the blue to finish.

■ **Mini DH line, 450 metres.** This trail, again close to the car park, is natural feeling with some techy bits and some larger features and gaps, so be aware the first time you ride it. It runs parallel to Bazza's Berms, and is also designed to be sessioned.

■ **Orange Loop 2.5 km.** This is a smooth and flowy jump line. It's as jumpy as you want to make it. The only gaps can be avoided; jumps get progressively bigger down the trail.

Other features

There is also a pump track and a skills area with red and black sections. It's built nicely for progression. There's even a tiny green loop for all ages.

MORAY MONSTER TRAILS

57.6131, -3.0758 / Fochabers, Moray, IV32 7PG (for the Winding Walks car park) / *forestryand-land.gov.scot/visit/moray-monster-trails*

57.6054, -3.0994 / Ordiquish Road, Fochabers, Moray, IV32 7PE (for the Ordiquish car park)

There are two trailheads here. Which you start from will depend on which trails you fancy riding or whether you want to pay for parking – essentially, the blues start from the tiny car park at Ordiquish (free) and the reds from Winding Walks car park (pay and display). There is also a connecting underpass below the A96 linking the two trailheads.

Trails
From Ordiquish:

■ **The Soup Dragon, 4.1 kilometres.** The Soup Dragon takes you from the car park to a central fire road running through the forest. You then have several options to add on to your ride, or alternatively you can head back to the trailhead. Going a bit further up the fire road means you can add the lovely descent of Dragon's Tail to your return. Going further will allow you to add Gordzilla and/or The Haggis as well. All of them have fun singletrack sections mixed in with a lot of fire road. It's complicated to describe, but flexible in practice and should give you a ride of the length you fancy.

🟦 **Gordzilla, 5.3 kilometres.** This gives an alternative way back to the start, or you can link it to the red trails via the underpass. It's a similar mix of singletrack and fire roads to the Soup Dragon.

🟦 **The Haggis, 8.8 kilometres.** This loops off into the forest to give a longer section of singletrack and fire roads, bringing you back to where you came off the fire road at the top end of the Soup Dragon.

From Winding Walks:
🟥 **The Fochabers Ring, 8 kilometres.** This is an XC-style route with a lot of fire road in between the singletrack. The singletrack is pleasant but not overly technical. The trail sections all have Lord-of-the-Rings-themed names, too. This is a good beginner red.

🟧 **Fochabers Freeride.** This is accessed from the red trail. It's slightly curiously named, but there are some North Shore features at the top of the trail and a few drops and jumps on the second half. There are a few line choices and roots to catch you out. It was all built by volunteers.

LEARNIE RED ROCKS. © ANDY McCANDLISH

Other features
🟧 **Skills area.** These are fun sections of varying difficulty, and are handily near the Winding Walks trailhead for a warm-up.

SANQUHAR WOODLANDS

57.5958, -3.6118 / Sanquhar Mains Private Road, Forres, Moray, IV36 2US / *forrescommunitywoodlands.org/sanquhar-woodlands-mountain-bike-trails*

Sanquhar Woodlands is a community woodland with short trails that allow sessioning. It's a great little local resource.

Trails
🟦 **Sanquhar Sanction, 1.1 kilometres.** This is a flowing trail making the most of the land. It's a lot of fun.
🟥 **Mannachie Mania, 250 metres.** This comes off the blue and adds drop-offs and rocks to the fun.
🟧 This is a line with even bigger drop-offs. It runs parallel to the blue and includes a jump line.

ABRIACHAN KELPIES' TRAILS

57.3852, -4.4303 / Abriachan, Inverness, Highland, IV3 8LB / *www.abriachan.org.uk/bike-trails*

This is a community-owned woodland with trails aimed mostly at beginners and families; it is an absolute little gem. It's great for improving basic skills. There are also some pretty good views on a nice day.

It's pretty much on the Great Glen Way if you fancy a diversion on a long-distance route. Abriachan Forest Trust always welcomes volunteers to help with trail maintenance.

SCOTLAND

LEARNIE RED ROCKS. © ANDY McCANDLISH

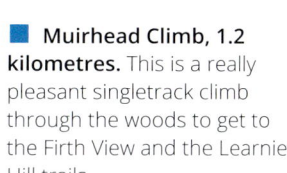

LEARNIE RED ROCKS. © ANDY McCANDLISH

Trails

 **3 kilometres.** This starts from the car park by the Abriachan Forest Trust classroom, and is a good introduction to off-road riding. It's wide, easy singletrack suitable for getting a feel for the place.

 **5 kilometres.** This starts from the second car park or it can be linked to the green route or the access road from the first car park. Comprising undulating and flowy singletrack and the odd technical feature, it's suitable for many riders.

■ **4 kilometres.** These trails come off the blue route – everything is short enough to make loops if you want to session stuff or not miss anything out. These add some extra tech but nothing overly scary. Combine with the blue for good progression.

Other features

■ There's also a skills area and a small jump park.

LEARNIE RED ROCKS

57.6246, -4.1173 / A832, Fortrose, Highland, IV10 8SL / *forestryandland.gov.scot/visit/learnie-red-rocks*

There are several trails here, all linked by fire roads; this arrangement does mean it's fairly easy to session stuff. One blue trail and the black trail are over a minor road. Check the trail map to see how you want to link them. There's plenty here to have a fun day out.

There's also a small fun dirt jump area near the car park and a couple of unsanctioned trails.

Trails

■ **Home Run, 500 metres.** A short introduction to mountain biking with accessible singletrack and easy/rollable jumps. It's downhill all the way after a climb on fire road to the start.

■ **Muirhead Climb, 1.2 kilometres.** This is a really pleasant singletrack climb through the woods to get to the Firth View and the Learnie Hill trails.

■ **Firth View Trail, 2 kilometres.** This trail involves a climb to a viewpoint and then flowy singletrack.

■ **Callachy Blue, 3.2 kilometres.** Another pleasant singletrack climb followed by a flowy blue descent, with rollers and tiny doubles that can be rolled or sent.

■ **Callachy Red Rocks, 1.2 kilometres.** A fun downhill with plenty of berms and jumps; optional black features.

■ **Learnie Hill, 3.6 kilometres.** This is tight, twisty and gnarly in places.

■ **Bike Park, 1.2 kilometres.** This has berms and jumps all the way down. The easier lines can be rolled. It's great for progression.

161

THE DIRT DIRECTORY

BALBLAIR

57.9033, -4.3569 / A836, Bonar Bridge, Highland, IV24 3AA / *forestryandland.gov.scot/visit/balblair*

This is a small forest with a small handful of biking and walking trails. There are toilets and a cafe in Bonar Bridge. At the time of writing (autumn 2024), sections of the black trail are closed for forestry work, but it appears they will reopen.

Trails
■ **5 kilometres.** This trail is about half and half fire road and singletrack. It is straightforward and pleasant, with wide, surfaced paths and a bit of fairly easy up and down.

■ **7.2 kilometres, plus 2.5 kilometres** on fire roads to get to the start. Expect a lot of glaciated bedrock and up and down, plus boardwalk in between the slabs. There's some more straightforward singletrack later on before some more rock slabs.

GOLSPIE – HIGHLAND WILDCAT

57.9767, -3.9802 / Rhives, Golspie, Highland, KW10 6SD / *www.highlandwildcat.com*

The big trail here is the one right from the top of Ben Bhraggie which is a contender for the longest purpose-built descent in Scotland, but there are also other, less demanding trails plus ways to make shorter loops. There are toilets and cafes in the village.

Trails
■ **13.6 kilometres.** The main trail is 13.6 kilometres long with a 5.2-kilometre climb on purpose-built trail with a few technical features. Then there is 1.3 kilometres of fire road to the Duke of Sutherland monument and incredible views. The Duke of Sutherland commemorated here wasn't the nicest of people, and was responsible for creating a lot of hardship during the Highland Clearances, so it's a controversial subject for a monument.

The views are worth riding up for, though. There are about 400 vertical metres of ascent, so be prepared for the weather at the top of Ben Bhraggie to be somewhat different to that in the village. After a breather, point down and enjoy over 5 kilometres of black-graded descent. It's varied and fun, although it is not the smoothest of tracks, so it will feel a very long way on a hardtail. It starts off with a section on the open hill, with drops and rocky chutes, before heading into the woods where it becomes a bit more like a trail centre. Be prepared. Some features will be worth looking at on your first ride down as it's far too easy to build up a lot of speed. The lower section is graded red.

If you don't fancy going all the way to the top or the weather is bad, there are ways to cut across the hillside from the ascent to the descent: Black Lynx is the highest way across, only cutting off the fire road ascent up and round Ben Bhraggie; Treeline cuts across at the treeline to take in the lowest part of the black descent; Red Lynx is the lowest of the trails across and means you can make a 6.7-kilometre red loop from the car park using the red-graded part of the descent.

LEWS CASTLE GROUNDS

58.2119, -6.3924 / Lews Castle Grounds, Stornoway, Isle of Lewis, Na h-Eileanan an Siar, HS2 0XS / *www.trailforks.com/region/castle-grounds-13238*

If you live in or for some strange reason happen to be near Stornoway with a mountain bike, there are a few trails here – though nothing particularly exciting – in the castle grounds.

Trails
There are about 11 kilometres of built trails through the castle grounds. Some are shared paths but there are some blue descents and one red one. There is also some off-piste stuff built by the locals. The tracks here are pleasant but not difficult riding, with good views over Stornoway.

NORTHERN IRELAND

To those not living there, it may come as a bit of a surprise exactly how much mountain biking there is in Northern Ireland, and that's despite open public access to mountains and hills being even more restricted than it is in England and Wales. However, even if you just stick to the trail centres mentioned here, there's plenty to have a go at. It's a great biking destination for a short break.

1. Blessingbourne *p168*
2. Gortin Glen *p168*
3. Davagh Forest *p169*
4. Garvagh Forest *p169*
5. Gosford Forest Park *p169*
6. Rostrevor *p170*
7. Tollymore *p170*
8. Castlewellan *p171*
9. Barnett Demesne *p171*

ROSTREVOR. © SHUTTERSTOCK/DELAYED PLEASURE

THE DIRT DIRECTORY

GORTIN GLEN FOREST PARK. © *SHUTTERSTOCK/WIRESTOCK CREATORS*

BLESSINGBOURNE

54.3848, -7.3097 / Blessingbourne Estate, Murley Road, Fivemiletown, County Tyrone, BT75 0QS / www.mountainbikeni.com/blessingbourne

While these trails are on a private estate and there is a charge for parking, the trails themselves are free to ride. This is not the hilliest place, so expect to do lots of pedalling.

Trails
■ **5 kilometres.** On one side of the road the blue and red trails share a fair amount of track. Some sections are also shared with other users, so be aware. It's a good flowing trail with some beginner trail features included. It's also possible to go back round to session your favourite sections, or to miss bits out if you need to cut it shorter.
■ **11 kilometres.** This is still primarily flowy, but with a few more technical features as well. The section across the road from Blessingbourne House is all classed as red. This isn't a particularly hard red, so if you got on okay with the blue (which makes up part of the 11 kilometres), you should be able to deal with this. The odd technical features can be bypassed or even walked.

Other features
■ **Pump track.** This is small but fun.

GORTIN GLEN

54.6840, -7.2465 / Glenpark Road, Omagh, County Tyrone, BT79 7SU / www.mountainbikeni.com/gortin-glen-forest-park

The trails here aren't so much rounds as various options linked together by fire roads – pretty much all of the climbing is on fire road. However, the official trails were only opened in 2020, so there is more to come. All of the trails seem to involve twisty singletrack – perfect, if that's your thing.

Trails
■ **7.1 kilometres.** This trail involves a fire road climb and then a choice: descend down the swoopy flow trail of Rollercoaster or climb a bit more and then head down Kelan's Chase, again swoopy and twisty.
■ **6.5 kilometres.** This comprises a fire road climb and then the tight, twisty singletrack of The Mountain and Sika's Run, or alternatively you can use the blue to follow River Run. There's nothing overly technical on any of the trails, so as long as you are good at cornering they are great for building up to red trails.

NORTHERN IRELAND

DAVAGH FOREST

54.7197, -6.9229 / Davagh Road, Omagh, County Tyrone, BT79 8JH / *www.mountainbikeni.com/davagh-forest*

There is a pretty reasonable range of trails in terms of difficulty at Davagh Forest, although there are quite a few fire road sections to join the good bits.

Trails

🟦 **7.5 kilometres.** This trail features sections of flowy singletrack in the trees linked by (sadly too much) fire road. There are occasional rocky features at the sides of the trail, which can be ridden or avoided. Higher up the hill, there are a couple more constructed trails that are on Trailforks but not the trail map. Further funding will hopefully be available to continue development.

🟥 **16 kilometres.** This takes the blue climb and then has a long fire road drag to get to the start of the good stuff. After the singletrack called Beleevna there is a split in the red trail: left takes you down Big Wig Jig, Giant's Bed and lots of twisty, undulating singletrack before you get to the interesting bedrock features of Boundary Rock – there are several lines here and it's worth sessioning. Going right after Beleevna takes you down Wolf's Hill and Run Ragley Run, which also have twisty, undulating singletrack aplenty. Both trails then join back in and follow the blue route back with a couple more red options, including more challenging bedrock sections at Eagle's Rock.

Multi-use trails

🟩 **3 kilometres.** Shared with walkers.

Other features

🟧 Pump track and skills park.

GARVAGH FOREST

54.9792, -6.6889 / Garvagh, Coleraine, County Londonderry, BT51 5NJ / *www.visitcausewaycoastandglens.com/things-to-do/garvagh-forest-trails-p749241*

This is a small wood which has walking trails as well as some shorter biking trails – be aware of other users. It's good for a quick, pedally blast or a gentle start for beginners.

You might not expect there to be a pyramid here, but there is. It was built as a burial chamber in the 19th century, but wasn't used.

Trails

🟦 **2.8 kilometres.** A gently flowing loop through the wood on fairly natural-feeling trails. There are some rollers and berms.

🟥 **4.7 kilometres.** This is a continuation of the blue, with a few more features thrown in. It's not overly technical.

🟧 **1.3 kilometres.** This is a skills loop aiming to test skills on the way to the main trails. There are various features such as berms and small drop-offs.

Multi-use trails

🟩 **1.3 kilometres.**

GOSFORD FOREST PARK

54.3072, -6.5129 / Markethill, Armagh, County Armagh, BT60 1GD / *getactiveabc.com/facility/gosford-forest-park*

Gosford Forest Park is aimed more at family group activities rather than mountain biking. It's also a place where *Game of Thrones* was filmed. There are walking trails and a pony trail, so be aware of other users on the shared-trail sections.

Trails

🟦 **8 kilometres.** This is a smooth, flowy trail with occasional features such as berms, rollers and drop-offs. It's good for beginners and families. There are a couple of optional slightly harder sections.

Multi-use trails

🟩 A short fire road ride.

Other features

🟧 Pump track.

THE DIRT DIRECTORY

ROSTREVOR. © RICHARD BARSON

ROSTREVOR

54.0977, -6.1857 / Shore Road, Rostrevor, County Down, BT34 3AA / *www.mountainbikeni.com/rostrevor* / Uplift: *www.bikemourne.com/rostrevor-mountain-bike-uplift*

This is the biggest and gnarliest of the Northern Irish trail centres, and there's not really anything for beginners. It has hosted the Red Bull Foxhunt, and there is fairly regular racing of the DH/enduro variety. You'll need to be fit and reasonably confident on a bike to make the most of the place, but if you are then there is some great riding here.

Trails

■ **27 kilometres.** This involves a long, steep, fire road climb to the start then some meandering singletrack, followed by a mix of fire road and singletrack climbing. There is a lot of climbing, making this route a challenge for those that aren't fairly fit: it's about 8 kilometres to the top, which is approximately 400 metres above sea level. Sorry, but that climb is pretty much unavoidable: no sweat if you're on an ebike, obviously. The views are amazing once you're up and then there's miles of singletrack, mostly downwards, with a variety of features such as the odd rock garden, drop and boardwalk. Plus, more amazing views. There's an optional black, which is rockier and more technical, that comes off Batt out of Hell. Overall, it's a big ride in terms of distance, height gained and potential exposure up top – be prepared. Careful reading of the trail map will allow you to cut it shorter using the fire roads if you need to.

■ **19 kilometres.** This follows the same huge red climb up before splitting off partway down the first red descent. It offers a rockier, more technical way of getting back down the hill before joining back into the red.

■ **Mega Mission DH, 1.8 kilometres.** This involves big jumps and big berms – lots of potential air time. It is more on the freeride side of DH.

■ **On the Pulse DH, 1.3 kilometres.** This is rockier, rootier and more technical than Mega Mission. It's more on the side of enduro/DH.

TOLLYMORE

54.2232, -5.9639 / 32 Hilltown Road, Bryansford, Newcastle, County Down, BT33 0PZ / *www.mountainbikeni.com/trail/tollymore-skills-course*

At the Tollymore National Outdoor Centre there is a 1.5-kilometre skills loop with a range of features which are the only sanctioned trails. It's also close to Tollymore Forest Park.

Trails

The 1.5-kilometre trail here is entirely singletrack, and packs in a lot of features for its short length, including berms, drop-offs, rollers, tabletops and North Shore.

NORTHERN IRELAND

CASTLEWELLAN

54.2608, -5.9520 / Castlewellan, County Down, BT31 9BU / www.mountainbikeni.com/castlewellan

This is another old estate, although the Victorian castle, built in the Scottish baronial style, is now a conference centre. There's also the National Arboretum, originally started in the 1850s with rare and unusual trees, and the Peace Maze, one of the world's largest permanent hedge mazes. In terms of the biking, there's a good variety of trails for many abilities.

ROSTREVOR. © RICHARD BARSON

Trails
■ 4.5 kilometres. This comprises gentle, flowing singletrack and some forest road around the lake. It's a good trail for beginners as a step up from the green.
■ 19 kilometres. This follows the blue trail out but then continues on flowy singletrack. It's not that technical, so is a good option for those wanting to try a red trail. Because of the way it loops round, there are plenty of opportunities to cut the ride short if needed. There are also plenty of ups and downs in the elevation profile, so it's nicely varied rather than straight up and down. Expect to pedal.
■ **The Great Escarpe and Dolly's Chute.** These are black options that come off the red trail, although the Great Escarpe does involve fire road to get to it. Both are a little rockier and a little more techy than the red trail, but this is more XC black than shredding the gnarr, with manufactured rock gardens and the odd drop every so often. Neither trail is purely down, but undulates in parts.

Multi-use trails
■ 4 kilometres. This loops around the lake.

Other features
■ Pump track. This is small and fun.

BARNETT DEMESNE

54.5485, -5.9705 / Belfast, County Antrim, BT9 5PR / www.mountainbikeni.com/barnett-demesne-trails-jumps-park

Barnett Demese is also known as Mary Peters trails/dirt jumps after the Olympian who has given her name to Northern Ireland's premier athletics track that is also at Barnett Demesne (hands up if you remember her; if you don't, look her up). This is a fab spot which is close to the city, especially due to the jumps – the first purpose-built jump spot in Ireland.

Trails
■ 3.9 kilometres. This is a fairly gentle wooded single-track which can get muddy in places. It's fabulous for kids and beginners.
■ 1.5 kilometres. Three extra trails come off the blue trail for a bit of added fun. There are some small trail features, but nothing too terrifying or techy.

Multi-use trails
■ 3.4 kilometres. A shared path.

Other features
■ Jump park. There are six lines of jumps here, varying from small ones to reasonably large doubles which are trick-able. It's nicely progressive: you can work up from rollers to tables to gaps. This is a great little jump spot which is well used by all ages.

GLOSSARY

Berm – a banked corner which allows you to corner without really losing speed.

DH – short for downhill. Designed for people who like pushing their bike to the top of the hill and then only riding it down. Due to the bigger nature of the suspension on a DH rig, DH-style trails tend to the steep and gnarly because the bikes can cope; they're not great on the flat or climbs.

Double – a jump with two lumps, which can either be sent as one jump (like a gap) or rolled.

Enduro – is the sort-of-easier cousin to DH. The bikes are easier to manoeuvre and are nearly as capable at handling rough ground. It's still primarily a style of getting to the bottom of a hill as fast as possible. Enduro-style trails tend to be reasonably techy.

Flow – a flowy trail is generally smooth and fast, possibly with jumps, but the emphasis is on being able to maintain speed. Expect berms to help you maintain pace.

Gap – a feature in a trail with a gap in it that cannot be avoided, and needs you to skilfully propel yourself, and your bike, over it. Landing short does not usually end well.

Gnarly – also 'shredding the gnarr' – this tends to be used to describe a trail that is just a little out of your comfort zone. It quite often involves rocks, roots and line choice.

Jump line – a trail designed specifically for getting your wheels off the ground. It may include tables and/or doubles. If you ride many of these, expect people to start talking to you about shark fins, kickers and steepness of lips. You may also be asked, 'Did you get your back end out much?' It's a whole separate lexis.

Mincing – riding a trail tentatively or unconfidently, braking too much and generally being in a mild state of terror. Friends can be encouraged down trails with calls of, 'Come on, yer mincer', or 'More mince than Tescos!' There's even a song: for those who remember the 1980s and Flashdance, you can fit the words, 'She's a mince-iac, mince-iac on the trail, and she's mincing like she's never minced before', to the tune of 'Maniac'. It's this sort of supportive behaviour which means your biking friends are your best friends.

Natural – obviously there are no 'natural' trails – someone has built that for you. But not all trails are surfaced and may retain more of the local woodland feel to them. These trails tend to change lots in different weather conditions.

Rollable – theoretically, this means that your bike will roll over features without you having to jump or drop them. However, there comes a point where it's technically trickier to roll something than jump it. And there can be a very personal definition of what can be

GLOSSARY

GRENOSIDE. © *JOHN COEFIELD*

classed as rollable or not. It's a never-ending source of debate.

Rooty, aka rooty goodness – a trail with lots of tree roots at the surface. Conventional wisdom says to try to hit them square on, but unfortunately roots don't always grow square across the track, which can make things trickier. They are worse when wet. Just try to relax and hope your bike picks up traction again before you make contact with the floor.

Sniper roots – these are the roots you don't see; they just have you on the ground unexpectedly before you even realise you've hit one.

Spooning – getting a jump all wrong, so instead of landing smoothly, you spoon.

Tabletop or table – a jump with a flat top, like a table, so if you land short it's not disastrous. Probably. The idea is to land on the downslope.

Techy – a trail quality that requires you to think and process the trail quickly. Expect rocks, roots and constant questions about line choice. Some people love this stuff, others avoid it.

XC – short for cross-country, which is mostly how mountain biking started. XC trails at trail centres are usually fairly tame as they tend to be a bit old school now. However, if an XC course has been built for a world cup expect something brutally steep and technical.

173

TOP TENS

A VARIETY OF TRACKS FOR DIFFERENT STANDARDS OF RIDERS

Sometimes you need to go somewhere that is going to cater for more than just your standard style of riding. Is there that one friend who constantly likes to ride a grade higher than your comfort zone? Have you brought the family and suddenly realise they are all much better than you are now? Go somewhere where there's a variety of tracks, and you can all have the ride you like and meet up afterwards with everyone happy.

1. **Tweed Valley** – Glentress especially (Scotland, *p135*)
2. **BikePark Wales** (Wales, *p103*)
3. **Forest of Dean Cycle Centre** (South West England, *p40*)
4. **Coed y Brenin** (Wales, *p115*)
5. **Comrie Croft** (Scotland, *p143*)
6. **Chicksands Bike Park** (Midlands & East Anglia, *p52*)
7. **Rogate Downhill B1KEPARK** (South East England, *p20*)
8. **Glenlivet** (Scotland, *p158*)
9. **Kirroughtree** (Scotland, *p128*)
10. **Isle of Wight Mountain Bike Centre** (South West England, *p35*)

EASY REDS

These places have red-grade trails that aren't too red, so are good for trying out the grade. Alternatively, you can easily try part of a trail.

1. **Thetford Forest** (Midlands & East Anglia, *p56*)
2. **Tunstall Forest** (Midlands & East Anglia, *p57*)
3. **Sherwood Pines** (Midlands & East Anglia, *p50*)
4. **Haldon Forest Park** (South West England, *p35*)
5. **Coed Llandegla** (Wales, *p118*)
6. **Cwmcarn** (Wales, *p107*)
7. **Carron Valley** (Scotland, *p140*)
8. **Hopton Wood** (Midlands & East Anglia, *p46*)
9. **Castlewellan** (Northern Ireland, *p171*)
10. **Mabie** (Scotland, *p131*)

SERIOUS GNARR SHREDDING

So, you like it steep and technical? Try these.

1. **Dyfi Bike Park** (Wales, *p111*)
2. **Antur 'Stiniog** (Wales, *p121*)
3. **Tweed Valley – Innerleithen and the Golfie** (Scotland, *p135*)
4. **Comrie Croft** (Scotland, *p143*)
5. **Nevis Range** – Top Chief and the DH track (Scotland, *p147*)
6. **BikePark Wales** (Wales, *p103*)
7. **Revolution Bike Park** (Wales, *p116*)
8. **Danny Hart's Descend Bike Park** (Northern England, *p91*)
9. **Glencoe Mountain Resort** (Scotland, *p145*)
10. **Gawton Gravity Hub** (South West England, *p32*)

TOP TENS

BIKEPARK WALES. © ANDY LLOYD/BIKEPARK WALES

JUMPS
Places to get some serious air time.
1. **Phoenix Bike Park** (Midlands & East Anglia, *p55*)
2. **S4P B1KEPARK** (South East England, *p22*)
3. **Woody's Bike Park** (South West England, *p30*)
4. **Old Hill Bike Park** (South West England, *p32*)
5. **Twisted Oaks Bike Park and Trails** (Midlands & East Anglia, *p56*)
6. **Bull Track Bike Park** (South East England, *p23*)
7. **Pimbo Bike Park** (Northern England, *p83*)
8. **Barnett Demesne** (Northern Ireland, *p171*)
9. **Dirt Farm** (Wales, *p107*)
10. **Wind Hill B1KEPARK** (South West England, *p38*)

STARTING OFF ON PROPER TRAILS
These places may have trails classed as blue, but they are great trails for everyone, from beginners through to the confident rider.
1. **Forest of Dean Cycle Centre** – Verderers Trail (South West England, *p40*)
2. **Haldon Forest Park** – Kiddens Trail (South West England, *p35*)
3. **Whinlatter** – Quercus Trail (Northern England, *p88*)
4. **Glentress** (Scotland, *p135*)
5. **Cannock Chase Forest** (Midlands & East Anglia, *p48*)
6. **Queen Elizabeth Country Park** (South East England, *p20*)
7. **Moray Monster Trails** (Scotland, *p159*)
8. **Cardinham Woods** (South West England, *p32*)
9. **Afan Forest Park** – Blue Scar (Wales, *p100*)
10. **BikePark Wales** (Wales, *p103*)

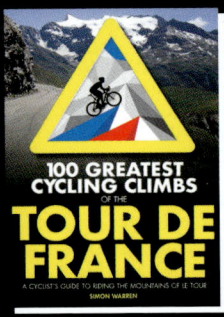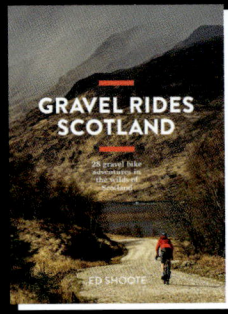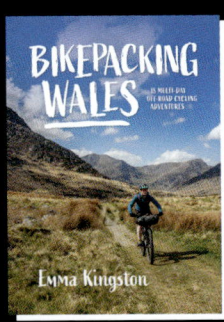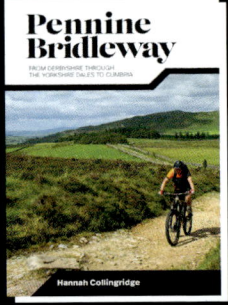